Nurturing Equanimity

Nurturing Equanimity

Building a Caring Culture

Michael Edmondson, PhD

BEP
BUSINESS EXPERT PRESS
Leader in applied, concise business books

Nurturing Equanimity: Building a Caring Culture

Copyright © Business Expert Press, LLC, 2023.

Cover design by Michael Edmondson

Interior design by Exeter Premedia Services Private Ltd., Chennai, India

First published in 2023 by
Business Expert Press, LLC
222 East 46th Street, New York, NY 10017
www.businessexpertpress.com

ISBN-13: 978-1-63742-502-2 (paperback)
ISBN-13: 978-1-63742-503-9 (e-book)

Business Expert Press Human Resource Management and Organizational Behavior Collection

First edition: 2023

10 9 8 7 6 5 4 3 2 1

Description

Nurturing Equanimity: Building a Caring Culture provides a much-needed blueprint for organizations looking to create a calm, balanced, and focused environment, inviting people to thrive in both their personal and professional lives.

This blueprint of nurturing equanimity to build a culture that cares is a necessity for any organization concerned about identifying, recruiting, and retaining the human capital required to create a sustainable future in today's post-COVID marketplace. Securing the right people for any organization is difficult in most markets; doing so as the economy emerges from the pandemic-induced global recession challenges even the most satisfied workplace cultures. The pandemic's disruption and residue created an unstable and imbalanced culture across organizations of all sizes and in each industry that exposed numerous negative workplace characteristics many either knew or never stopped to consider.

Examples included low wages, long and unnecessary commutes, bad management, and unfulfilling work. These characteristics were symbolic of organizational cultures, outdated, toxic, and imbalanced, created by incompetence, inertia, and ineptitude. The pandemic allowed employees to pause, consider their life situation, and realize their lives had been imbalanced for far too long.

Required reading for individuals from small-to-medium sized businesses, large corporations, nonprofit organizations, and government offices, *Nurturing Equanimity: Building a Culture That Cares* offers employers and employees alike a valuable resource to use as they chart a course forward in a postpandemic marketplace.

Keywords

business culture; organizational culture; leadership; business; organization; equanimity; employees; management

Contents

Other Books by Edmondson

Agility: Management Principles for a Volatile World
Embracing Ambiguity: A Workplace Training Plan for the
PostPandemic Economy
Major in Happiness: Debunking the College Major Fallacies
Marketing Your Value: 9 Steps to Navigate Your Career
Strategic Thinking and Writing
Success: Theory and Practice
The Relevance of Humanities to the 21st Century Workplace

All titles are available at Amazon and https://www.businessexpertpress
.com/michael-edmondson/

Testimonials

*"*Nurturing Equanimity *clearly explains how 'being nice' to employees not only makes sense but makes good business sense. An easy read that can help an organization gain longevity from their employees during this challenging human resource market we are experiencing."*—**Walter Nugent, Chair, Fire Science Department, New Jersey City University**

"Michael Edmondson returns to the post pandemic recovery with another great book. Nurturing Equanimity: Building a Caring Culture *is a must read for executives, graduate students, and anyone aspiring to embrace diversity, equity, and inclusion head on. His book will help you build a caring culture that will make any organization prosper."*—**Mike Provitera, Executive Leadership Trainer**

"Dr. Michael Edmondson has built a practical step-by-step program to encourage and challenge organizations to shift the cultural paradigm towards equanimity. A balance of professional and personal well-being is critical in our post-pandemic environment; Dr. Edmondson has created a well-defined blueprint for success. As a resilience professional, I support his call to action and applaud his evidence-based approach."—**Nichol Killian, DSocSci, Certified Trauma Support Specialist (CTSS), Certified Resilience Professional (CRP)**

Introduction

The residue of the COVID-19 global pandemic will continue to impact how we work, live, and do almost everything else in the near future. The previous model for understanding the long-lasting impact of a global health crisis was the 1918 H1N1 flu pandemic, often referred to as the "Spanish flu," which killed an estimated 50 million people worldwide and approximately 675,000 people in the United States.[1] If the 1918 flu pandemic exists today, over a century later, it may be reasonable to expect that COVID-19 will follow a similar course. Both pandemics destabilized markets, governments, businesses, and individuals on an unprecedented scale with the exception of the two world wars.[2] The destabilization of COVID-19 continues to ripple across the United States as millions of people have altered the course of their life or work. Such alterations developed during the lockdown periods of the COVID-19 pandemic when working and schooling from home became the only option and, as a result, people discovered the value of nurturing equanimity, finding balance in their life, and exploring the possibilities of their life that existed beyond what they thought was "normal."

Researchers Joan P. Ball and Julia Beck labelled those moments when people confront disruption in their careers as inflection points. Navigating the professional and personal residue of the COVID-19 pandemic created an unsure, unsettling, and unfamiliar terrain. Ball and Beck noted how creating a habit of pausing to regulate, resource, and reorient before responding can counteract the threat response. Such a process can instil

---

[1] D. Jordan. n.d. "The Deadliest Flu: The Complete Story of the Discovery and Reconstruction of the 1918 Pandemic Virus," Centers for Disease Control and Prevention. www.cdc.gov/flu/pandemic-resources/reconstruction-1918-virus.html.
[2] S.R. Fox-Dichter, Y. Chun, and M. Grinstein-Weiss. November 23, 2021. "The Destabilizing Cost of a Pandemic: What COVID-19 Meant for Renters Already Getting Assistance," The Brookings Institute. www.brookings.edu/blog/up-front/2021/11/23/the-destabilizing-cost-of-a-pandemic-what-covid-19-meant-for-renters-already-getting-assistance/.

a sense of curiosity and creativity in the face of uncertainty."[3] Nurturing equanimity allows individuals to pause and reorient prior to responding. Creating balance in one's life provides those necessary moments of clarity amidst the chaos. "Making time to assess the new landscape," according to Ball and Beck, "can help us to shift our attention from the threat of the unknown toward inquiry as we enter unchartered territory."[4] *Nurturing Equanimity: Building a Caring Culture* is designed to help leaders, managers, and everyone else navigate the unchartered territory of the near future as COVID-19 subsides and shifts into the background of subtle permanence.

In a series of 10 chapters, *Nurturing Equanimity* walks individuals through a series of steps to implement should they be interested in building a caring culture. Doing so involves a recalibration of how the office works, how employees communicate with one another, and how management creates a culture focused on balance while maintaining an emphasis on organizational sustainability. The landscape demands that everyone think differently. But thinking is arduous work and often makes people uncomfortable. When people are uncomfortable, they tend to shy away from doing what is necessary to grow. Embracing the ambiguity of today's unchartered territory by nurturing equanimity and building a caring culture offers organizations a vibrant approach as they look to remain relevant in today's dynamic, ever-changing, and hypercompetitive global marketplace.

As McKinsey noted in an April 13, 2022 Executive Briefing: "Sustainable, inclusive growth will require changing the workplace to maximize the contributions of all people. Each sector, industry, and function will have to reinvent itself to achieve maximum growth and sustainability."[5] In 2022, of the approximately eight billion humans on this

---

[3] J.P. Ball and J. Beck. May 16, 2022. "You've Reached an Inflection Point in Your Career. What Now?" *Harvard Business Review.* https://hbr.org/2022/05/youve-reached-an-inflection-point-in-your-career-what-now?ab=hero-subleft-2.

[4] Ibid.

[5] McKinsey. April 13, 2022. "COVID-19: Implications for Business," Briefing note#100. www.mckinsey.com/business-functions/risk-and-resilience/our-insights/covid-19-implications-for-business.

planet, about 3.3 billion of them worked in organizations. With over three billion people working in organizations around the world, individuals are being shaped both directly and indirectly by the organizational culture. As McKinsey noted in its *2023 State of Organizations* report "Getting organizations right, even at a time when the very definition of 'being at work' is in a state of flux, is thus not just about individual companies and institutions: it's about the broader well-being of society."[6] Only time will tell if leaders can reinvent themselves and create a new workplace culture that, in turn, helps spark a much-needed period of sustained growth. Nurturing Equanimity provides 10 chapters of one plan, as there are others, for those willing to invest in creating a caring culture.

Chapter 1 explains the market realities and is a necessary first step in creating a caring culture. Managers interested in nurturing equanimity need to help their people understand the present-day marketplace characteristics. Doing so ensures everyone is on the same level of understanding as to the elements affecting the ongoing disruption. Chapter 2 examines the strategic imperatives necessary for any organization to remain vital, vibrant, and sustainable today. While each organization will have strategic imperatives relevant to its mission, this chapter details some of the more common ones across industries, locations, and markets. Chapter 3 helps people understand the link between professional development and personal growth. Often overlooked, misunderstood, or ignored, it is imperative that if one wants to grow as a leader, one must also develop as a person. Chapter 4 defines equanimity so that any organization or leader can articulate a clear, concise, and compelling message. Since communication is the foundation for any caring culture, a shared definition of equanimity is paramount for any organization looking to nurture it. Chapter 5 examines the place of self-care in today's workplace. As discussed throughout this publication, many people leave their current place of employment due to its toxicity and lack of concern for workers' self-care.

---

[6] McKinsey, *The State of Organizations, 2023: Ten Shifts Transforming Organizations,* April 26, 2023. https://www.mckinsey.com/capabilities/people-and-organizational-performance/our-insights/the-state-of-organizations-2023

Chapter 6 discusses the two paradigms of mindfulness. Like Chapter 4 that defines equanimity, this sixth chapter helps leaders understand the difference between mindfulness in the east and how the west has altered its original meaning. Chapter 7 outlines the necessity of being consistent and positive as a leader. Creating a caring culture relies on a consistent application of positive energy; this is especially true during stressful period where the organization needs to navigate the chaos and find a way forward. Chapter 8 explains the role of a growth mindset and how that is involved with creating a caring culture. Leaders with fixed mindsets seldom possess the flexibility of thought, the ability to invite multiple perspectives, or the capacity to collaborate, all of which are necessary to nurture equanimity and build a caring culture. Chapter 9 highlights a seldom discussed concept in the world of business, but a necessary one nonetheless, and this is impermanence. If millions of people quitting their jobs during the last two years has taught leaders anything, it is the reality that employees have reminded themselves they have the capacity to leave at any time. Finally, Chapter 10 compliments the impermanence discussed in the previous chapter and focuses on unattachment. To truly nurture equanimity and create a caring culture, leaders need to help their people understand that not only is everything temporary in this world but also that no one should become so attached to a job that it has a negative impact on their ability to engage in self-love, self-care, and self-respect.

If nurturing equanimity and building a caring culture seems overwhelming, then you are not alone. Creating an organizational culture in today's postpandemic global marketplace presents a vast number of challenges for even the most skilled leader and manager. For those most committed, however, it may help to recall the words of Liz Coleman in her 2009 TED talk when she discussed the work involved with processing being overwhelmed. Good leaders, those concerned about their people at the human level, are most likely overwhelmed these days as they struggle to build a caring culture. For Coleman, she reminds leaders everywhere "you have two things. You have a mind. And you have other people. Start with those and change the world."[7]

---

[7] L. Coleman. 2009. "A Call to Reinvent Liberal Arts Education," TED. www .ted.com/talks/liz_coleman_a_call_to_reinvent_liberal_arts_education/transcript.

Kelly Williams, senior vice president and chief human resources officer for the Blue Cross Blue Shield Association, went further and stressed the need for self-awareness.[8] For Williams, self-awareness, when combined with how well people care for themselves mentally and physically while at work and in life, influences everything. In a March 2, 2021, interview, Williams said: "I would love to see equanimity as a core competency in schools. At the heart of it, it is about being grounded and centered amidst the chaos. Like all skills, it requires practice."[9] My wish is that this publication, in some small way, contributes to the discussion around nurturing equanimity and creating a caring culture so that organizations can remain vital, vibrant, and relevant as individuals around the world engage in the self-care required to live a more engaging, fulfilling, and thriving life.

---

[8] M. Lieberman. March 2, 2021. "Top U.S. Companies: These Are the Skills Students Need in a Post-Pandemic World," *Ed Week*. www.edweek.org/technology/ top-u-s-companies-these-are-the-skills-students-need-in-a-post-pandemic-world/ 2021/03.

[9] M. Lieberman. March 2, 2021. "Top U.S. Companies: These Are the Skills Students Need in a Post-Pandemic World," *Ed Week*. www.edweek.org/technology/ top-u-s-companies-these-are-the-skills-students-need-in-a-post-pandemic-world/ 2021/03.

CHAPTER 1

Explaining the Market Realities

In his May 7, 2022 *Fast Company* article, DocuSign CEO Dan Springer noted that he, along with so many other leaders, initially misjudged the lasting employment changes wrought by the pandemic.[1] One of the most significant market realities he learned to acknowledge over time was the Great Resignation, the Great Reshuffling, or the Great Renegotiation, where millions of people quit their jobs, left one opportunity for a better one, or renegotiated their current work situation. Greg Rosalsky and his National Public Radio (NPR) colleagues spoke with Karin Kimbrough, the chief economist of LinkedIn, who observed, "There are twice as many jobs on our platform as there were a year ago; and with so many open jobs workers have greater power to negotiate a better position."[2] It took Springer a while, but he ultimately realized how "the pandemic awakened in the global workforce a renewed desire for meaning, balance, and responsibility in both work and life."[3] The pandemic allowed people to catch their breath from the daily commute and in so doing they realized how the old paradigm of "working for the weekend" was far from an optimal way of living. Springer acknowledged how during the post-COVID period employees were rightfully demanding more. Meeting the evolving

---

[1] D. Springer. May 7, 2022. "Coming to Grips With the Seismic Shift in Our Work and Our Lives," *Fast Company*. www.fastcompany.com/90747635/coming-to-grips-with-the-seismic-shift-in-our-work-and-lives.

[2] G. Rosalsky. January 25, 2022. "The Great Resignation? More like The Great Renegotiation," *NPR*. www.npr.org/sections/money/2022/01/25/1075115539/the-great-resignation-more-like-the-great-renegotiation.

[3] D. Springer. May 7, 2022. "Coming to Grips With the Seismic Shift in Our Work and Our Lives," *Fast Company*. www.fastcompany.com/90747635/coming-to-grips-with-the-seismic-shift-in-our-work-and-lives.

needs of employees will be no easy task for organizations. Failure to do so, however, according to Springer could result in the loss of "the world's best and brightest talent. Not acting quickly and definitively is an unthinkable proposition."[4]

Nurturing Equanimity: Building a Caring Culture is designed to help leaders act quickly and definitively so they can identify, retain, and develop employees and remain relevant in today's hypercompetitive, dynamic, and ever-changing global marketplace. This first chapter defines the three market realities related to building a caring culture: (1) people experiencing an existential crisis, (2) employees realizing the need for balance among their personal and professional lives, and (3) organizations starting to nurture equanimity.

Leaders across all industries should also acknowledge the market reality explained in the observation by Laura Barton that "the pandemic encouraged many to perform an emotional audit of their lives."[5] This unplanned period of reflection provided individuals with a respite from their entrenched routine. An unintended consequence of COVID's lock down permitted people to recalibrate their work/life balance and also helped them realize "life is perhaps too short to spend doing something you do not love."[6] For example, one woman reported how the forced stoppage of her normal routine during the pandemic provided personal reflection time as well as a better understanding of others and her need to demonstrate compassion and empathy.[7] This period of pandemic-induced self-reflection has a long history in the United States. The value of self-awareness was first etched in Americana by the 19th-century naturalist, poet, and philosopher Henry David Thoreau who uprooted

---

[4] Ibid.

[5] L. Barton. May 7, 2022. "'I Yearned for a Deeper, Slower, More Useful Existence:' Dispatches From the Great Resignation," *The Guardian*. www.theguardian.com/books/2022/may/07/i-yearned-for-a-deeper-slower-more-useful-existence-dispatches-from-the-great-resignation.

[6] Ibid.

[7] P. van Kessel, C. Baronavski, A. Scheller, and A. Smith. March 5, 2021. "In Their Own Words, Americans Describe the Struggles and Silver Linings of the COVID-19 Pandemic," *Pew Research Center*. www.pewresearch.org/2021/03/05/in-their-own-words-americans-describe-the-struggles-and-silver-linings-of-the-covid-19-pandemic/.

his life and went into the woods because he "wished to live deliberately, to front only the essential facts of life."[8] Such a deliberate placement into the woods would, Thoreau believed, help him learn perhaps the most valuable lessons life has to offer. The poet philosopher did not want to discover at the time of his death that he did not live for he "did not wish to live what was not life, living is so dear."[9]

The search for meaning, regardless of the century, is nothing new, as humans have a fundamental need to perceive life as meaningful. Such a need stems from the feeling that one's existence has purpose and significance. The pandemic, however, resulted in a lockdown that forced people to spend time alone or with their loved ones at a greater rate than before the crisis. This significant amount of time gave employees the opportunity to deeply reflect on their work and how it impacts their personal lives. As individuals conducted this life audit, they came to realize that they have the ability to live a life they want; not what some manager dictates.[10] For example, a Pew Research Center study reported how the pandemic reminded people of the critical role relationships play in life. Instead of being drown out by the noise of the daily commuting and working grind, the pandemic induced travel ban reminded people of the importance of relationships by showing them what life is like when they cannot spend time with loved ones or showing what life is like when they have the opportunity to spend more time them.[11]

Elise Gould, senior economist at the Economic Policy Institute, also recognized the ripple effect emotional and life audits had in creating this new market reality and wrote "I certainly think that the pandemic has led many people to reevaluate their work and their priorities and what they

---

[8] H.D. Thoreau. n.d. Wikipedia. https://en.wikipedia.org/wiki/Henry_David_Thoreau (accessed May 9, 2022).

[9] Ibid.

[10] L.R. Roepe. n.d. "The Employee Experience," *Society for Human Resource Management.* www.shrm.org/hr-today/news/all-things-work/pages/the-employee-experience.aspx.

[11] P. van Kessel, C. Baronavski, A. Scheller, and A. Smith. March 5, 2021. "In Their Own Words, Americans Describe the Struggles and Silver Linings of the COVID-19 Pandemic," *Pew Research Center.* www.pewresearch.org/2021/03/05/in-their-own-words-americans-describe-the-struggles-and-silver-linings-of-the-covid-19-pandemic/.

want to do."[12] Barton observed "if we are lucky, all of us are given a moment to question the narrative of our lives. To wonder whether where we find ourselves is the result of our own choices, or of convention and others' expectations."[13] Research published by the University of Michigan in February 2022 echoed similar sentiment. According to the study's lead author, Erin Cech, associate professor of sociology at the University of Michigan, "the emphasis on finding passion in one's work suggests that employment instability can spark existential unsettling that leads people to broader senses of meaning-making beyond financial stability."[14] In other words, the emotional audit undertaken by millions of workers gave them an opportunity to experience an existential disruption in their lives where they placed purpose-driven work over salary and benefits.

In "Why the COVID-19 Pandemic Has Caused a Widespread Existential Crisis," Jamie Ducharme noted this existential disruption and clarified that those who made a major personal or professional shift during the pandemic had a level of privilege over those who lost their job, a loved one, or suffered a health crisis. For Ducharme, "The COVID-19 pandemic appears to have spurred a collective reckoning with our values, lifestyles and goals—a national existential crisis of sorts."[15] While anxiety, in general, is part of the human experience, the level felt during the pandemic transcended the typical stress about life prior to the global health crisis. The emotional audit and existential crisis experienced by so many during the pandemic generated a widespread unease about meaning,

---

[12] E. Segal. January 12, 2022. "How Companies Can Respond to the Rising Tide of the Great Resignation," *Forbes*. www.forbes.com/sites/edwardsegal/2022/01/12/how-companies-can-respond-to-the-rising-tide-of-the-great-resignation/?sh=727f67c973d5.

[13] L. Barton. May 7, 2022. "'I Yearned for a Deeper, Slower, More Useful Existence:' Dispatches From the Great Resignation," *The Guardian*. www.theguardian.com/books/2022/may/07/i-yearned-for-a-deeper-slower-more-useful-existence-dispatches-from-the-great-resignation.

[14] University of Michigan press release. February 1, 2022. "Career Priorities Emphasize Passion Over Financial Security During Pandemic." https://news.umich.edu/career-priorities-emphasize-passion-over-financial-security-during-pandemic/.

[15] J. Ducharme. December 29, 2020. "Why the COVID-19 Pandemic Has Caused a Widespread Existential Crisis," *Time*. https://api.time.com/wp-content/uploads/2020/12/covid-life-decisions.jpg.

choice, and freedom in life.[16] It is normal to experience an existential crisis from time to time, especially after a life event, such as the death of a loved one, the diagnosis of a serious health issue, or a significant birthday. Often viewed as a journey, a necessary experience, or a complex phenomenon, an existential crisis stems from the self-awareness that your life will end one day and that mystery, unfamiliarity, and discomfort have replaced any sense of perceived normalcy. Assessing the impact of an existential crisis, Katherine King observed the necessity of engaging in the self-care required to patiently process one's emotions. Only after a period of such patience King noted, "can people let themselves feel their emotions and make space for new perspectives" as they begin the process of moving forward.[17]

When people process their existential crisis, they leverage their minds, body, and spirit on what makes their lives fulfilling. As Clay Routledge noted "meaning reduces existential anxiety and helps someone feel like they're part of something larger and longer lasting than their brief, mortal lives."[18] Therein lies the impact of the pandemic; it allowed people around the world to slow down and reassess their life situation. Noting the transformational power of an existential crisis, King acknowledged the pain associated with such a life moment. Like a storm one needs to weather, this pain can "offer wisdom, hope, and profound positive transformation" for those willing to put in the work required to grow. "By being patient, curious, and willing to act, we can carry ourselves safely through to a better and more meaningful tomorrow."[19] The disruption within the employment market exemplifies how the existential crisis

---

[16] S. Johal. January 29, 2021. "Covid Is an Existential Crisis That Comes From an Awareness of Your Own Freedoms," *The Guardian*. www.theguardian.com/world/2021/jan/30/covid-is-an-existential-crisis-that-comes-from-an-awareness-of-your-own-freedoms.

[17] K. King. January 31, 2002. "Coping With an Existential Crisis," *Psychology Today*. www.psychologytoday.com/us/blog/lifespan-perspectives/202101/coping-existential-crisis.

[18] C. Routledge. June 7, 2021. "You Can't Cure Your Employee's Existential Crisis. But You Can Help," *Harvard Business Review*. https://hbr.org/2021/06/you-cant-cure-your-employees-existential-crisis-but-you-can-help.

[19] K. King. January 31, 2002. "Coping With an Existential Crisis," *Psychology Today*. www.psychologytoday.com/us/blog/lifespan-perspectives/202101/coping-existential-crisis.

of the pandemic resulted in a better and more meaningful tomorrow for millions of people.

Once individuals started to conduct an emotional audit of their life, or merely an assessment of their life situation, that led to the second market reality where millions changed their employment position. Anthony Klotz, a professor at Mays Business School in Texas, coined this change that millions of workers were undertaking during the pandemic as "the Great Resignation" and suggested this market reality would continue into the near future as the world adjusted to the ripple effects of the pandemic. He echoed Barton's observation about an emotional audit people undertook of their lives and wrote "during the pandemic, people spent time doing different things, whether with family or hobbies and came to the realization 'I'm more than just my job.'"[20] In a March 13, 2022 *Fast Company* article, Joseph Andrew, global chairman of Dentons, the world's largest law firm with more than 20,000 people in 81 countries, suggested that the Great Resignation is perhaps better viewed through the lens as that of a Great Transition. According to Andrew "People of varying backgrounds, places and circumstances are looking for something different than what they have now."[21] The self-reflection so many people engaged in during the pandemic provided them with the realization that transitioning to a new and more meaningful work culture was indeed possible. "This Great Transition" as Andrew labeled it "is a key attribute of a new dynamic, an environment shaped by constant and rapid change, where there will never be a new normal."[22]

To substantiate Klotz's hypothesis and Andrew's observation, in March 2022, a record 4.53 million workers quit their jobs, beating the previous series high of 4.51 million in November 2021, according to the Job Openings and Labor Turnover Survey (JOLTS) released by the

---

[20] A. Klotz. n.d. Interview. www.theversemedia.com/articles/anthony-klotz-defining-the-great-resignation

[21] J. Andrew. March 13, 2022. "The Employee-Employer Disconnect That's Fueling the Great Resignation," *Fast Company*. www.fastcompany.com/90728005/the-employee-employer-disconnect-thats-fueling-the-great-resignation.

[22] Ibid.

U.S. Department of Labor's Bureau of Labor Statistics.[23] While it is true that millions of people quit their jobs each year prior to the pandemic, the new reality is that the quit rate since the pandemic has exceeded earlier levels. Statista, a market and consumer data website, published research results and found "The number of Americans quitting has now exceeded prepandemic highs for eight straight months, as employers, especially in low-wage sectors, are struggling to fill open positions."[24] As Anneken Tappe reported for CNN Business on February 1, 2022, "A record number of 47.4 million workers, more than a quarter of the total workforce, quit their jobs in 2021 while US employers had more positions to fill than ever before; over 10 million."[25] While there are many reasons for this new market trend, "one major driver appears to be that many workers are no longer willing to put up with the pay and/or working conditions they (perhaps grudgingly) accepted prior to the pandemic."[26]

In a blog post explaining the ongoing resignation of millions of workers, ClearStar, a technology company specializing in background screening, published a blog post and suggested many factors were contributing to the resignations such as low pay, no benefits, a lack of professional growth opportunities, too long of a commute, or some combination of them. To improve the organizational health and culture, "employers should listen to employees, understand their career desires, and work on developing lasting relationships with employees to help prevent people from leaving."[27] Tracey Malcolm, global leader of the future of work and risk at Willis Towers Watson (WTW), observed that "some people are

---

[23] U.S. Bureau of Labor Statistics. May 3, 2022. "Job Openings and Labor Turnover—March 2022." www.bls.gov/news.release/jolts.nr0.htm.

[24] F. Richter. January 11, 2022. "The Great Resignation," *Statista*. www.statista .com/chart/26186/number-of-people-quitting-their-jobs-in-the-united-states/.

[25] A. Tappe. February 1, 2022. "A Record Number of Americans Quit Their Jobs in 2021," *CNN*. www.cnn.com/2022/02/01/economy/us-job-openings-quite-december/index.html.

[26] Ibid.

[27] ClearStar. November 29, 2021. "The Great Resignation of 2021." www.clear star.net/the-great-resignation-of-2021/.

leaving for a nudge up in pay, but some are not."[28] In the consulting firm's *2022 Global Benefits Attitudes Survey*, WTW discovered 20 percent of the employees surveyed reported they would take a new job for the same pay. The report found that the post-COVID employee, given the time to reflect, now considered factors other than wages such as health benefits, job security, flexible work arrangements and retirement benefits as key drivers of employee satisfaction.[29]

Instead of viewing the mass exodus of millions away from their current employment position as a Great Resignation, Springer labeled such a movement as the "Great Embrace." The pandemic allowed individuals an opportunity to embrace what really matters in life: family, community, and craft.[30] The life assessments individuals engaged in during the pandemic helped them pause and reflect on their levels of stress, many of which identified with increased levels. Gallup polls, for example, found that workers' life evaluations have declined during the pandemic (regardless of remote/in-person work) and that 61 percent of women and 52 percent of men feel stressed on a typical day, both up from before the pandemic.[31] The American Psychological Association found similar results in its research and discovered in its *2021 Work and Well-being Survey* of 1,501 U.S. adult workers, 79 percent of employees had experienced work-related stress in the month before the survey, 36 percent reported cognitive weariness, 32 percent reported emotional exhaustion, and an astounding 44 percent reported physical fatigue—a 38 percent increase since 2019.[32]

---

[28] G. Iacurci. March 22. "The Great Resignation Continues, as 44% of Workers Look for a New Job," *CNBC*. www.cnbc.com/2022/03/22/great-resignation-continues-as-44percent-of-workers-seek-a-new-job.html.

[29] Ibid.

[30] D. Springer. May 7, 2022. "Coming to Grips With the Seismic Shift in Our Work and Our Lives," *Fast Company*. www.fastcompany.com/90747635/coming-to-grips-with-the-seismic-shift-in-our-work-and-lives.

[31] L. Saad, S. Agrawal, and J. Rothwell. March 22, 2021. "Life Evaluation Slips More for U.S. Working Women Than Men." https://news.gallup.com/poll/340898/life-evaluation-slips-working-women-men.aspx [news.gallup.com].

[32] A. Abramson. January 1, 2022. "Burnout and Stress Are Everywhere," *American Psychological Association*. www.apa.org/monitor/2022/01/special-burnout-stress.

With increased levels of stress part of today's reality, and to better understand why people were quitting their jobs, *The Hustle* published the results of a survey of over 1,000 employees who left their jobs during the pandemic. The findings, released in March 2022, found the following:[33]

- ~27 percent of respondents left because they found a job with better pay. That reason was followed by:
  - Finding a more rewarding job (~17 percent)
  - Burnout (~17 percent) (Note: Burnout afflicted people of all professions. Respondents in the service-industry and blue-collar sectors were about as likely to say they were burned out as people in white-collar industries.)
  - Pursuing a new career path (10 percent)
  - Lack of flexible work atmosphere (8 percent)
  - Starting a business (6 percent)
- 64 percent of respondents switched to a new job immediately, and 83 percent of them made more money at their new job.

Klotz's own research echoes that of *The Hustle* and found "many resignations have been driven by psychological factors: to cure burnout or focus on caregiving responsibilities."[34] Again, such findings would have been difficult to acknowledge, had it not been for the COVID induced lock down and time away from commuting to the office. Additionally, Klotz noted a common transformation among employees in that many said "their life revolved around work before the pandemic and coming out of it, they want work to adjust to their life."[35]

One related characteristic of this market reality is that both the U.S. economy and housing market flipped from recession into expansion

---

[33] M. Dent. March 12, 2022. "Why People Are Really Leaving Their Jobs During the Great Resignation," *The Hustle*. https://thehustle.co/why-people-are-really-leaving-their-jobs-during-the-great-resignation/.

[34] M. Smith. March 17, 2022. "Experts Share the No. 1 Pandemic Work Trend They Think Will Stick Around," *CNBC*. www.cnbc.com/2022/03/17/experts-share-the-no-1-pandemic-work-trend-they-think-will-stick-around.html.

[35] Ibid.

by the summer of 2020. From the summer of 2020 to the spring of 2022, the U.S. housing boom witnessed prices soar 34.4 percent.[36] The number of Americans who moved in 2021 jumped 20 percent above 2020 levels as approximately 23 million people chose to relocate to places that accommodated new pandemic-era lifestyles, such as the new work-from-home options some employers instituted.[37] "As data roll in for April–May 2022, however, it is clear that the pandemic housing boom is cooling as the national economy recalibrates itself to a postpandemic environment."[38]

Another new market reality an organization needs to communicate before nurturing equanimity and building a caring culture is the realization that some companies are starting to pay attention to how their employees are responding to the emotional audit they underwent during the pandemic. As Morgan Smith observed, "the Covid-19 pandemic triggered a historic quitting spree that has forced companies to re-think not just where to work, but how to improve the employee experience."[39] Findings from a 2021 LinkedIn survey published in April 2022 confirmed Smith's observations. To attract and retain talent, the LinkedIn survey found that companies have begun to respond to new requests from employees. For example, some organizations are starting to offer more opportunities to get promoted and gain new skills to increase flexibility. In the post-COVID workplace, such changes "have put employees and job seekers in the driver's seat, igniting them to rethink what they expect out of an employer today."[40] The emotional audit and existential

[36] L. Lambert. May 26, 2022. "The Cooling Housing Market Enters Into the Great Deceleration," *Fortune.* https://fortune.com/2022/05/26/the-cooling-housing-market-enters-into-the-great-deceleration/.

[37] T. Bove. May 2, 2022. "These Are the Cities Everyone Wants to Move to Right Now, According to a Top Relocating Company," *Fortune.* https://fortune.com/2022/05/02/penske-cities-everyone-wants-to-move-to-in-2022/.

[38] L. Lambert. May 26, 2022. "The Cooling Housing Market Enters Into the Great Deceleration," *Fortune.* https://fortune.com/2022/05/26/the-cooling-housing-market-enters-into-the-great-deceleration/.

[39] M. Smith. April 6, 2022. "Amazon Is the No. 1 Company to Work for in 2022, According to LinkedIn," *CNBC.* www.cnbc.com/2022/04/06/amazon-is-the-no-1-company-to-work-for-in-2022-according-to-linkedin.html.

[40] "Top Companies 2022: The 50 Best Workplaces to Gow Your Career in the U.S." April 6, 2022. LinkedIn. www.linkedin.com/pulse/top-companies-2022-50-best-workplaces-grow-your-career-us-/.

crisis made one aspect of modern work rather clear; many people found a renewed emphasis of meaning over money.

Interestingly enough, this trend of meaning over money started to emerge pre-COVID. As Gallup discovered in its 2015 research, "even when workplaces offered benefits such as flextime and work-from-home opportunities, engagement predicted wellbeing above and beyond anything else. Employees prefer workplace wellbeing to material benefits."[41] Employee well-being is defined by Gallup as a component of the following five characteristics: purpose (liking your work), social (supportive workplace relationships), financial (earning a competitive salary), community (having pride in your community), and physical (having good health and energy). What exactly is the relationship between culture and employee well-being? As Emma Seppälä and Kim Cameron proclaimed in the *Harvard Business Review*, "Wellbeing comes from one place, and one place only—a positive culture."[42] The pandemic paused any sense of well-being for some time as managers navigated the chaos of the global marketplace. Now that the world has started to emerge, postpandemic organizations are once again trying to figure out how to nurture a caring culture that promotes employee well-being.

As Clay Routledge wrote in the *Harvard Business Review*, in the post-COVID environment "managers should look beyond salary and other material benefits and think about what is going to help workers meet their need for meaning in life."[43] For example, the dating app Bumble and the career networking site LinkedIn each took a week off to help their employees recharge. Canadian e-commerce company Shopify instituted "Rest & Refuel Fridays" globally during the 2021 summer. Additionally, Fidelity is granting U.S. full-time and part-time employees five additional paid "relief days" for unexpected events, as well as elder and child

---

[41] D. Witters and S. Agrawal. October 27, 2015. "Well-Being Enhances Benefits of Employee Engagement," *Gallup*. www.gallup.com/workplace/236483/enhances-benefits-employee-engagement.aspx.

[42] E. Seppälä and K. Cameron. December 1, 2015. "Proof That Positive Work Cultures Are More Productive," *Harvard Business Review*. https://hbr.org/2015/12/proof-that-positive-work-cultures-are-more-productive.

[43] C. Routledge. June 7, 2021. "You Can't Cure Your Employee's Existential Crisis. But You Can Help," *Harvard Business Review*. https://hbr.org/2021/06/you-cant-cure-your-employees-existential-crisis-but-you-can-help.

care coordinators to help identify caregivers or tutors. The fund manager also expanded a program to help parents of children with behavioral or developmental disabilities.[44] Marriott International is adding three paid "TakeCare Days Off" on the Fridays before Memorial Day, July Fourth, and Labor Day for nonhotel staffers. The world's largest hotel chain also "strongly encourages teams" to avoid all meetings on Fridays. If a critical meeting must take place, "we ask that it be concluded by no later than noon, local time," Sarah Brown, Marriott's director of corporate media relations wrote in an e-mail. [45]

While these perks may seem to assuage the new concerns expressed by employees, leadership teams should realize that research published in September 2021 by McKinsey found that many workers view such efforts as transactional. "This transactional relationship, however, reminds employees that their real needs aren't being met."[46] Noting the emotional audit millions of workers engaged in during the pandemic, McKinsey observed "Employees are tired, grieving, and want a renewed sense of purpose in their work."[47] The Pew Research Center survey echoed such sentiment and concluded that "managers should expect a post-pandemic workforce that is more focused on the fulfillment they get from time spent with loved ones."[48] In a February 2022 *Forbes* article, Spencer Hadelman, CEO at Advantage Marketing, emphasized the need for companies and organizations to "prioritize employee wellness and a healthy work-life

---

[44] S. Youn. June 29, 2021. "America's Workers Are Exhausted and Burned Out-and Some Employers Are Taking Notice," *Washington Post*. www.washingtonpost.com/business/2021/06/28/employee-burnout-corporate-america/.

[45] Ibid.

[46] A. De Smet, B. Dowling, M. Mugayar-Baldocchi, and B. Schaninger. September 8, 2021. "'Great Attrition' or 'Great Attraction'? The Choice Is Yours," *McKinsey Quarterly*. www.mckinsey.com/business-functions/people-and-organizational-performance/our-insights/great-attrition-or-great-attraction-the-choice-is-yours.

[47] Ibid.

[48] P. van Kessel, C. Baronavski, A. Scheller, and A. Smith. March 5, 2021. "In Their Own Words, Americans Describe the Struggles and Silver Linings of the COVID-19 Pandemic," *Pew Research Center*. www.pewresearch.org/2021/03/05/in-their-own-words-americans-describe-the-struggles-and-silver-linings-of-the-covid-19-pandemic/.

balance."[49] Instead of the usual and customary cultural traits of a hybrid remote work environment and unlimited Paid Time Off (PTO), employees who have worked through their existential crisis now demand more from their managers today. To address the demands of the postpandemic workforce, Hadelman suggests that leaders "should be regularly checking in with their team to gauge their workload and overall happiness."[50]

Organizations that nurture equanimity and build a caring culture in the near future recognize the profound sense of wanting to be valued demonstrated by employees in the post-COVID marketplace. In addition to social and interpersonal connections with their colleagues, employees post-COVID want to feel a sense of "shared identity as well as meaningful—though not necessarily in-person—interactions, not just transactions."[51] Leaders who nurture equanimity and build a caring culture have an opportunity to offer individuals more than transactions; they can intentionally provide transformational work. This shift from transaction to transformation will form a key characteristic of a culture, especially for those employees who engaged in an emotional audit or process an existential crisis during the pandemic.

Employees who have engaged in an emotional audit or existential crisis during the pandemic are bringing new demands to the workplace and organizations looking to thrive in today's hypercompetitive, dynamic, and ever-changing global marketplace need to make sure workers at all levels feel valued. Hadelman believes that "feeling valued leads to increased productivity and ultimately a happier and healthier work environment."[52] To help design such meaningful interactions,

---

[49] S. Hadelman. February 22, 2022. "Employee Retention Strategies To Implement In 2022," *Forbes.* www.forbes.com/sites/forbesagencycouncil/2022/02/22/employee-retention-strategies-to-implement-in-2022/?sh=3cba84994421.

[50] Ibid.

[51] A. De Smet, B. Dowling, M. Mugayar-Baldocchi, and B. Schaninger. September 8, 2021. "'Great Attrition' or 'Great Attraction'? The Choice Is Yours," *McKinsey Quarterly.* www.mckinsey.com/business-functions/people-and-organizational-performance/our-insights/great-attrition-or-great-attraction-the-choice-is-yours.

[52] S. Hadelman. February 22, 2022. "Employee Retention Strategies To Implement In 2022," *Forbes.* www.forbes.com/sites/forbesagencycouncil/2022/02/22/employee-retention-strategies-to-implement-in-2022/?sh=3cba84994421.

some organizations have started to promote an office culture that values unplugging from work. Doing so creates boundaries and balances professional and personal time.[53] As the global marketplace continues to emerge from the disruption caused by the pandemic, it will be imperative for managers to find new ways to build a culture that cares by nurturing equanimity and providing the meaningful interactions and balance employees are currently seeking.

Conclusion

This first chapter explained three market realities related to building a caring culture: People processed their existential crisis, employees placed a greater emphasis on balancing their personal and professional lives, and a few of the more progressive organizations have started to nurture equanimity. More needs to be done. Much more. Senior leaders across all industries need to remember the observation by Springer who made it clear that "employees will continue to look for more attractive, meaningful work" in the post-pandemic world. "They have made it clear where they'd like to go; it's up to us to meet them there."[54] Will your organization nurture equanimity and build a caring culture to provide attractive and meaningful work?

The prepandemic models of employee engagement and retention are simply not working. As highlighted by Matt Cain, CEO, Couchbase in a December 2021 *Inc.* article, management culture needed a reset and the pandemic exposed problems and accelerated change in areas that were recognized but rarely addressed.[55] In the post-COVID global marketplace marked by constant disruption, organizations should prioritize mission

---

[53] C. Routledge. June 7, 2021. "You Can't Cure Your Employee's Existential Crisis. But You Can Help," *Harvard Business Review.* https://hbr.org/2021/06/you-cant-cure-your-employees-existential-crisis-but-you-can-help.

[54] D. Springer. May 7, 2022. "Coming to Grips With the Seismic Shift in Our Work and Our Lives," *Fast Company.* www.fastcompany.com/90747635/coming-to-grips-with-the-seismic-shift-in-our-work-and-lives.

[55] M. Cain. December 2021. "How Leaders Can Help Employees Thrive in the 2022 Workplace," *Inc.* www.inc.com/matt-cain/how-leaders-can-help-employees-thrive-in-2022-workplace.html.

and people in every decision. Creating a caring environment demands management's vigilance in understanding the motivations and development goals of employees coupled with a daily commitment to building an exceptional culture of purpose and belonging.[56] Klotz echoed a similar sentiment and suggested how organizations and leadership teams "really need to think seriously about inclusivity and making sure employees can bring their whole selves to work—while also recognizing that you don't want employees for whom work is the only thing in their lives."[57] With this in mind, the second chapter explains the next step in the process of building a caring culture, that is, articulating the strategic imperatives of an organization.

---

[56] D. Springer. May 7, 2022. "Coming to Grips With the Seismic Shift in Our Work and Our Lives." *Fast Company*. www.fastcompany.com/90747635/coming-to-grips-with-the-seismic-shift-in-our-work-and-lives.

[57] A. Klotz. n.d. Interview. www.theversemedia.com/articles/anthony-klotz-defining-the-great-resignation.

CHAPTER 2

Articulating the
Strategic Imperatives

Now that the key market realities have been identified, this second chapter articulates the strategic imperatives organizations with caring cultures should focus on in order to create a sustainable, relevant, and vibrant future. Leaders who explain the market realities discussed in Chapter 1 set the stage to help their employees shift from global concerns to local ones. Strategic imperatives may differ among organizations across industries. Therefore, this second chapter includes those imperatives relative to organizations embracing equanimity to build a caring culture and a sustainable future. Prior to COVID, the more progressive, innovative, and forward-thinking organizations had started to become more agile, digital, and people centered. As Ernst & Young (EY) noted in 2021, however, "COVID-19 significantly accelerated that journey for all organizations on a scale they didn't dream about 12 months ago. Companies are actively taking this opportunity to transform their organizations with customers and employees at the center of their efforts."[1]

Author Daniel Coyle echoed a similar sentiment and observed "today's world is demanding more adaptability, more learning, and more malleability."[2] Such transformation is taking place throughout many organizations as leaders shift their strategic imperatives to "capture the upside of the economic rebound. Within this competitive context, CEOs not yet designing and delivering ambitious investment strategies for growth risk

---

[1] A. Guerzone, N. Mirchandani, and B. Perkins. January 2023. "CEO Outlook Pulse." *EY*. www.ey.com/en_eg/ceo.

[2] "Unleash Your Team's Full Potential." June 22, 2022. McKinsey Interview. www.mckinsey.com/featured-insights/mckinsey-on-books/author-talks-unleash-your-teams-full-potential.

falling behind in the race to transform for a better future."[3] Once a leader has set the stage for a nurturing equanimity and building a caring culture by outlining the market realities, they can then define the various strategic imperatives for their organization. Without articulating the organization's strategic imperatives in a clear, concise, and compelling manner, leaders risk the communication required to nurture equanimity and build a caring culture.

In *The Culture Playbook: 60 Highly Effective Actions to Help Your Group Succeed*, Daniel Coyle identified three pillars to an organization's culture. The first pillar is getting people to connect where the employees feel confident about the company's future and their future with the company. Creating situational awareness is the second pillar that involves building a culture of progress, not perfection. Finally, the third pillar is direction, as the leadership clearly articulates its purpose so everyone moves toward the same goal.[4] Defining the various strategic imperatives can help connect employees to the organization's future, understand that progress is better than perfection, and ensure that everyone is aware of the collective goal.

Like the other steps defined throughout this publication, this second element of clearly communicating the organization's strategic imperatives may require leaders to think differently. During the pandemic, many businesses and organizations were forced to adapt to new ways of working; especially in the early stages where lockdowns were imposed for extended periods of time. As the global marketplace started to open up in 2022 and leaders prepared for life in the post-COVID-19 era, they were made to realize the necessity of doing more than fine-tune their day-to-day tasks. Leaders who want their organization to remain vibrant, relevant, and vital also need to be ready and willing to rethink how they operate and even why they exist. To thrive in the post-COVID-19 era, leaders need to step back, pause, take a breath, and consider a broader perspective. In an interview from Motley Fool Live recorded on June 15, Udemy Chief Learning

---

[3] EY. January 10, 2022. "The CEO Imperative: Will Bold Strategies Fuel Market-Leading Growth?" www.ey.com/en_eg/ceo/will-bold-strategies-fuel-market-leading-growth.

[4] D. Coyle. 2022. *The Culture Playbook: 60 Highly Effective Actions to Help Your Group Succeed*. www.amazon.com/Culture-Playbook-Effective-Actions-Succeed/dp/0525620737.

Officer Melissa Daimler shared her thoughts on this necessary change required of leaders and culture in the post-COVID-19 era and emphasized the importance of workplace culture and how it has evolved over the past few years. "I think we realize over the last couple of years in this pandemic," Daimler explained, "that culture isn't conflated with what's necessarily at the office. In fact, we're doing ourselves a disservice if we think about culture like that."[5]

Before identifying the strategic imperatives driving the post-COVID-19 marketplace, it is critical to understand three facts revealed by research published in the Harvard Business Review. First, 85 percent of executive leadership teams spend less than one hour per month discussing strategy. Unfortunately, leadership teams allow themselves to get involved in tactical issues others should address. Second, on average, 95 percent of a company's employees don't understand its strategy. It is virtually impossible to build a caring culture if 95 percent of employees fail to understand the organization's strategy. Finally, as a result of the previous two findings it should come as no surprise then that 90 percent of businesses fail to meet their strategic targets.[6]

To nurture equanimity and build a caring culture, an organization must ensure that its leadership spend time discussing, assessing, and communicating its strategic imperatives and then effectively communicate them. In the post-COVID-19 era, leaders have a long way to go when it comes to articulating its strategic imperatives to its employees. To nurture equanimity and build a caring culture, "leaders today must assess how the company culture will potentially impact the strategy, and account for those internal barriers as part of the rollout process."[7] As the global marketplace continues to deal with the volatility, uncertainty, complexity, and ambiguity (VUCA) of life post-COVID, executive leadership teams who

---

[5] "Leaders Must Reshape Their Company Culture Framework, One Expert Explains." June 24, 2022. www.fool.com/investing/2022/06/24/leaders-must-reshape-their-company-culture-framewo/.

[6] C. Cote. October 6, 2020. "Why Is Strategic Planning Important?," *Harvard Business Review*. https://online.hbs.edu/blog/post/why-is-strategic-planning-important.

[7] A.B. Olson. June 24, 2022. "4 Common Reasons Strategies Fail," *Harvard Business Review*. https://hbr.org/2022/06/4-common-reasons-strategies-fail.

fail to commit to a "solid communication plan will leave employees with contradicting messages, customer experiences that lack follow-up, undefined processes, and a lack of direction across the entire organization."[8] Poor communication by leadership often has the opposite effect of creating a caring culture, often provides a negative experience for employees and consumers, and can also have a negative impact on profits.

To help leaders nurture equanimity and build a caring culture, this chapter examines a series of strategic imperatives centered around three guiding principles: agility, purpose, and trust. The hallmark of a caring culture where equanimity is nurtured remains agile in thought, focused on purpose, and serious about building trust with its customers and clients.

The Strategic Imperative of Agility

VUCA of the post-COVID global market presents new challenges, issues, and questions for leaders each day. To address these concerns, the leadership teams and cultures looking to remain vibrant, vital, and relevant today need to practice an agile mindset. Doing so can help create a caring culture and chart a path forward to sustainability. According to Gallup's research published in 2019, "Organizations that aren't agile and that don't have the capacity to adapt quickly will be overcome by their competitors—or put out of business."[9] In its 2019 *Global CEO Outlook* titled *Agile or Irrelevant: Redefining Resilience*, the consulting firm Klynveld Peat Marwick Goerdeler (KPMG) concluded: "A successful CEO is an agile CEO. Over two-thirds of chief executive officers believe that agility is the new currency of business. If they fail to adapt to a constantly changing world, their business will become irrelevant."[10] Moreover, McKinsey's

---

[8] "Improve Your Company Culture With The 3 Cs of Culture." June 22, 2022. Home Furnishing Association. https://myhfa.org/improve-your-company-culture-with-the-3-cs-of-culture/.

[9] J. Clifton and J. Harter. June 16, 2019. "It's the Manager: From Gallup, Based on the Largest Global Study on the Future of Work," SlideShare presentation. https://slideshare.net/ShivShivakumar1/book-summary-its-the-manager.

[10] KPMG. 2019. *Agile or Irrelevant: Redefining Resilience, 2019 Global CEO Outlook*. https://drive.google.com/file/d/1Q3aNiey6XPAaNyc-CbFReBQ10u CqZWk6/view.

research details how "the agile organization is dawning as the new dominant organizational paradigm. Rather than organization as machine, the agile organization is a living organism."[11] Agility is here to stay as long as the global marketplace keeps disrupting the way people live, work, and do just about everything around the world. Moreover, the emergence of the COVID-19 global pandemic during the completion of this book stressed organizations around the world and exposed significant issues, concerns, and problems. To address the pressure points made visible by the unexpected crisis, organizations looking to create a sustainable future had as their new priority "the making of meaningful investments in human capital to build an agile, flexible workforce."[12] As such, it is important to begin with a definition.

There are as many definitions of agility as there are people defining the word. The standard definition comes from the *Merriam-Webster's Dictionary*, which defines agility as "being agile" and agile as "marked by ready ability to move with quick easy grace or having a quick resourceful and adaptable character." The etymology of agile originates from Latin *agilis* and from *agere* "do." As the world went from a connected to a hyperconnected global economy during the last 15 years, agility became a focus point for business writers since managers needed to determine how best to navigate the dynamics driving the disruptive marketplace and *do* something. In Google Book's N Gram Viewer analysis, *agile* was barely mentioned from 1800 to 1995. The period from 1995 to the present marked a significant increase in the use of the word agile and the future trend continues upward.[13]

In *Agility: How to Navigate the Unknown and Seize Opportunity in a World of Disruption* (2019), Leo M. Tilman and General Charles Jacoby (Ret.) focused on the organization and defined agility as

---

[11] "The Five Trademarks of Agile Organizations." January 2018. *McKinsey Report*. https://mckinsey.com/business-functions/organization/our-insights/the-five-trademarks-of-agile-organizations.

[12] S. Tincher. July 1, 2020. "An Agile Workforce will Be Key to Success Post-Pandemic," *Market Insights*. https://benefitspro.com/2020/07/01/an-agile-workforce-will-be-key-to-success-post-pandemic/?slreturn=20200602083402.

[13] Google Books N Gram Viewer for agile available at https://tinyurl.com/ngramagile.

"The organizational capacity to effectively detect, assess and respond to environmental changes in ways that are purposeful, decisive and grounded in the will to win." In *Emotional Agility: Get Unstuck, Embrace Change, and Thrive in Work and Life (2016)*, Susan David broadened the definition of agility to include emotions and wrote: "Emotional agility—being flexible with your thoughts and feelings so that you can respond optimally to everyday situations-is a key to well-being and success." In *The Agility Shift: Creating AGILE and Effective Leaders, Teams, and Organizations* (2015), Pamela Meyer focused on what she labeled the agility shift: "The Agility Shift is the intentional development of the competence, capacity, and confidence to learn, adapt, and innovation in changing contexts for sustainable success." In *Leadership Agility: Five Levels of Mastery for Anticipating and Initiating Change* (2006), Bill Joiner and Stephen Josephs define agility as "the ability to take wise and effective action amid complex, rapidly changing conditions." They use the words leader and manager interchangeably and believe there are five levels to the agile leader: expert, achiever, catalyst, cocreator, and synergist and three functional areas of pivotal conversations, team leadership, and organizational leadership. Each examination into agility provides important points to consider in the ongoing dialogue. As organizations look to achieve and sustain growth in today's ever-changing landscape, the value of agility will only increase.

An organization that nurtures equanimity and creates a caring culture leverages its agility to "be more flexible, less hierarchical, and more diverse."[14] Additionally, organizations that practice an agile approach to problem solving provide themselves with opportunities to incorporate sustainability into their strategic plan. Sustainability is defined as the principle of producing goods and services while inflicting minimal damage on the environment. While some organizations have taken earnest steps in this regard already, doing so in the near future will be as fundamental to doing business as compiling a balance sheet since

---

[14] "What Matters Most." September 2021. McKinsey & Company. www.mckinsey.com/capabilities/strategy-and-corporate-finance/our-insights/what-matters-most-six-priorities-for-ceos-in-turbulent-times.

consumers and regulators will insist on it.[15] Caring cultures that adapt to the post-COVID market by leveraging an agile mindset are also demonstrating to their employees the organization's commitment to purpose.

The Strategic Imperative of Purpose

The search for purpose at work has existed for decades and well before the COVID-19 global pandemic fractured the world economy. For example, in a January 25, 1970 sermon published by "The Riverside Church" of New York City, Minister Ernest T. Campbell emphasized the place of purpose when he said: "It has been said that the two most important days of a man's life are the day on which he was born and the day on which he discovers why he was born."[16] Four years later, American author, historian, and broadcaster Studs Terkel published *Working: People Talk About What They Do All Day and How They Feel About What They Do* and echoed similar sentiment when he wrote, "I think most of us are looking for a calling, not a job. Most of us, like the assembly-line worker, have jobs that are too small for our spirit. Jobs are not big enough for people."[17]

For the discussion here, the word purpose will be used interchangeably with vocation. A precise definition of vocation can be found in the observation by British-American poet Wystan Hugh Auden, "You owe it to all of us to get on with what you're good at." The Japanese word that comes closest to resembling vocation is *ikigai* (pronounced Ick-ee-guy)—a reason to get out of bed each morning. The Japanese island of Okinawa, where *ikigai* has its origins, is said to be home to the largest population of centenarians in the world. In *Blue Zones: Lessons on Living Longer from the People Who've Lived the Longest*, Dan Buettner suggests that the practice of *ikigai* contributes to longevity. To identify *ikigai*, Buettner suggests

---

[15] Ibid.

[16] *Two Most Important Days in Your Life: The Day You Were Born and the Day You Discover Wh*. https://quoteinvestigator.com/2016/06/22/why/#f+13878+1+1.

[17] S. Terkel. 1974. *Working: People Talk About What They Do All Day and How They Feel About What They Do.*

making three lists: your values, things you like to do, and things you are good at. The cross-section of the three lists is your *ikigai*. Leaders who nurture equanimity and build a caring culture actively support employees who wish to pursue their *ikigai*.

Finally, leaders need to recognize that people want meaning in their lives and their work. Previous research has found that companies with a strong sense of purpose outperform those that lack one. And those who say they live their purpose at work are simply better employees—more loyal, more likely to go the extra mile, and less likely to leave. Purpose helps companies recognize emerging opportunities and connect with their customers.[18] Most organizations, however, have a long way to go when it comes to creating the modern structure required to nurture equanimity. For example, according to research conducted by the consulting firm Korn Ferry, "just 45% of companies have embedded purpose into their culture, and only 13% proactively campaign for issues related to their stated purpose."[19]

A Gartner survey of 3,500 employees around the world in October 2021 to determine the pandemic's impact on their personal and professional lives. According to the results, the pandemic had a direct impact on how many people reconsidered their purpose in life and work.[20] The soul searching that occurred during the pandemic created a seismic shift in people's attitudes, and as a result, the survey reported the following percentages of people agree or strongly agree with the statement "the pandemic…"

> …shifted my attitude toward the value of aspects outside work (65 percent)
> …made me rethink the place that work should have in my life (65 percent)

---

[18] S. Clark. 2022. "State of American Business 2022." www.uschamber.com/on-demand/economy/5-takeaways-from-suzanne-clarks-first-state-of-american-business-address.

[19] K. Ferry. n.d. "Future of Work Trends in 2022: The New Era of Humanity." www.kornferry.com/insights/featured-topics/future-of-work/2022-future-of-work-trends.

[20] J. Wiles. January 13, 2022. "Employees Seek Personal Value and Purpose at Work: Be Prepared to Deliver," *Gartner*. www.gartner.com/en/articles/employees-seek-personal-value-and-purpose-at-work-be-prepared-to-deliver.

…made me long for a bigger change in my life (62 percent)

…changed my perspective on the desirability of my workplace location (58 percent)

…made me want to contribute more to society (56 percent)[21]

Just how important is the post-COVID work emphasis on purpose, and what is its relationship to building a caring culture? Research from the site Great Place to Work indicates the following three questions will predict workplace turnover, regardless of generation or job type:

1. Are you proud of where you work?
2. Do you find meaning in your work?
3. Do you have fun at work?[22]

If someone answers "no" to one or more of those three questions, they are more than likely looking to leave the organization.[23] In the post-COVID environment, individuals want to spend their time in meaningful ways and have a renewed commitment to finding work with purpose so they can make a difference in the world. As employers continue to experiment with the right combination of work from home/work from office, one thing is certain, today's employees are searching for "a workplace that allows them to bring their whole selves to work, collaborate with colleagues, and have a bit of fun while doing it."[24] A caring culture offers the opportunity for leadership to give people workplace flexibility and freedom, provides purposeful work where innovation is encouraged, and hires only those who value purpose driven work in a caring and supportive environment. Once employees know their organization cares about them and provides purposeful work, there is a bond

---

[21] Ibid.

[22] R. Amire. May 10, 2022. "Purpose at Work Predicts If Employees Will Stay or Quit Their Jobs," *Great Place to Work.* www.greatplacetowork.com/resources/blog/purpose-at-work-predicts-if-employees-will-stay-or-quit-their-jobs.

[23] Ibid.

[24] C. Hastwell. July 16, 2021. "The 3 biggest Predictors of Employee Retention (Especially Millennials)," *Great Place to Work blog.* www.greatplacetowork.com/resources/blog/3-keys-to-millennial-employee-retention.

of trust created that, in turn, can help the organization remain vibrant, vital, and relevant.

The Strategic Imperative of Trust

For leaders of organizations nurturing equanimity and building a caring culture by relying on an agile mindset and providing purposeful work, they also understand the growing value of trust. Due to the political upheaval around the world during the last decade, trust is one commodity in short supply, especially when it pertains to the government and the media. The 2022 Edelman Trust Barometer is the organization's trust and credibility survey, which it has been conducting for 22 years. In its latest survey spanning over 36,000 respondents in 28 countries respondents reported "a world ensnared in a vicious cycle of distrust, fueled by a growing lack of faith in media and government. Through disinformation and division, these two institutions are feeding the cycle and exploiting it for commercial and political gain."[25] As a result of this growing distrust in government and the media, the Edelman Trust Barometer suggested the expectations of businesses to lead will increase. Such a function, however, will require "all institutions to foster innovation and drive impact.[26]

The strategic imperative of trust between businesses and nonprofit organizations is clear when:

- 58 percent of respondents would buy or advocate for brands based on their beliefs and values;
- 60 percent would choose a place to work based on their beliefs and values; and
- 80 percent would invest based on their beliefs and values.[27]

In addition to the Edelman Trust Barometer, the consulting firm PwC also conducted its own survey in August 2021 to explore trust by

---

[25] "2022 Edelman Trust Barometer: The Cycle of Distrust." n.d. www.edelman .com/trust/2022-trust-barometer.
[26] Ibid.
[27] Ibid.

surveying more than 500 business leaders and 1,000 consumers in the United States, the majority of whom are employed by U.S. companies.[28] Among PwC's findings were:

- 73 percent of business leaders cite the CEO as either responsible for or accountable for trust.
- 80 percent of employees trust their company the same or more now than before the pandemic.
- 49 percent of consumers started purchasing or purchased more from a company because of trust.[29]

In a June 15, 2022 LinkedIn post, U.S. Chair and Senior Partner at PwC Tim Ryan reinforced the strategic imperative of trust when he wrote, "The world is changing at an unimaginable pace, and leaders have to remain nimble while meeting expectations from a myriad of stakeholders. To thrive today and in the future, it takes trust."[30] To support his recommendation, Ryan referred to recent research that discovered how much business leaders overestimate the extent to which their employees and customers trust them. For example, recent Gallup research published in April 2023 noted "Only 21% of U.S. employees strongly agree that they trust the leadership of their organization."[31] Additionally, recent research also found a remarkable distinction between what business leaders think and the reality when it comes to trust. "Over 85 percent of business leaders think customers highly trust their companies when only about 30% of consumers do."[32] Moreover,

---

[28] "The Complexity of Trust: PwC's Trust in US Business Survey." n.d. www.pwc.com/us/en/library/trust-in-business-survey.html.

[29] Ibid.

[30] T. Ryan. June 15, 2022. "Trust: The New Currency for Business," LinkedIn. www.linkedin.com/pulse/trust-new-currency-business-tim-ryan/.

[31] D. McLain and R. Pendell. April 17, 2023. "Why Trust in Leaders Is Faltering and How to Gain It Back," *Gallup*. www.gallup.com/workplace/473738/why-trust-leaders-faltering-gain-back.aspx#:~:text=Employee%20Trust%20in%20Organizational%20Leadership&text=In%20the%20latest%20reading%2C%20from,the%20leadership%20of%20their%20organization.

[32] T. Ryan. June 15, 2022. "Trust: The New Currency for Business," LinkedIn. www.linkedin.com/pulse/trust-new-currency-business-tim-ryan/.

the PwC research identified a significant misalignment on what builds trust. Over 45 percent of executives say trust is built from customers, employees, and other stakeholders rather than senior leadership. But only 27 percent of customers and 35 percent of employees say the same, indicating that they are looking to the C-suite to lead more on trust. Such a gap, suggested Ryan, could have significant "consequences ranging from employee retention rates to the bottom line."[33]

Recent efforts to either gain or build trust appear to be paying off as both employees and customers report higher trust in U.S. businesses now than before the pandemic began. With trust in government and media so low, businesses can rise to the occasion and fill the tremendous trust gap that exists in the post-COVID environment. As with any progress, however, challenges still abound as many organizations have been slow to practice agility and provide the purpose-driven work required to gain trust. PwC concluded that the path forward to achieve the strategic imperative of trust is certainly possible for those business leaders who "think differently about their organization's big-picture trust strategy, their stakeholders' priorities, and their choice of trust initiatives."[34] Commenting on the strategic imperative of trust in a post-COVID world, U.S. Chair and Senior Partner of PwC Tim Ryan wrote in a February 2022 *Harvard Business Review* article:

> Our business community has come a long way in building trust with consumers and putting greater social needs in line with the responsibility to grow revenue. While it's a hill we are still climbing, we are capturing the opportunity to make positive, lasting change for our stakeholders and society-at-large—and that is a step in the right direction.[35]

---

[33] Ibid.

[34] "The Complexity of Trust: PwC's Trust in US Business Survey." n.d. www.pwc.com/us/en/library/trust-in-business-survey.html.

[35] T. Ryan. February 7, 2022. "How Business Can Build and Maintain Trust," *Harvard Business Review*. https://hbr.org/2022/02/how-business-can-build-and-maintain-trust.

Conclusion

Before concluding Chapter 2, it is important to shed light on one specific sector that is in dire need of identifying its strategic imperatives. According to the National Association of Nonprofit Organizations & Executives (NANOE) "a potentially extinction level event is occurring in the nonprofit sector. All nonprofit leaders are faced with critical decisions about the survival and well-being of their organization, staff, customers, and finances right now."[36] In a December 2021 article, NANOE noted that many nonprofit organizations across the United States have already made major changes in order to remain relevant, vital, and vibrant. For example, in a 2021 study focused on New Jersey, "78% of the nonprofits polled had canceled programs and/or events, 17% suspended all operations temporarily, and 27% laid off or cut staff."[37] For those trying to nurture equanimity and create a caring culture the suspension of operations, programs, and staff present even more challenges leaders need to address.

The pandemic has been a wake-up call for many leaders at for-profit businesses, nonprofit organizations, and government offices, and the transformation imperative is now clearer than ever. Today's volatile, uncertain, complex, and ambiguous (VUCA) leaders require an agile mindset coupled with a personality comfortable with embracing ambiguity if they hope to reconfigure their organizations and offices for resilience and investing boldly for optimal growth. But Executive Directors of nonprofit organizations and leaders across all sectors who are unable to take bold steps could face stern tests down the line, particularly as intensifying headwinds pose challenges in the race to capture emerging opportunities. The need to act now is too strong. CEOs who stand still will fall behind in the race for market-leading growth.[38]

---

[36] K. Robinson. December 25, 2021. "Nonprofits, Covid & 2022—Eight National Questions." https://nanoe.org/nonprofits-covid-2022-eight-national-questions/#.

[37] Ibid.

[38] EY. 2022. "Will Bold Strategies Fuel Market-Leading Growth?," *EY 2022 CEO Outlook Survey.* https://assets.ey.com/content/dam/ey-sites/ey-com/en_gl/topics/ceo/ey-ceo-survey-global-report-v2.pdf?download.

CHAPTER 3

Linking Personal and Professional Growth

While the first two chapters outlined how and why leaders should define the market realities (Chapter 1) and articulate the strategic imperatives (Chapter 2), this chapter explains the link between personal growth and professional development. If one wants to grow as a professional, one must engage in the requisite self-awareness work to grow as a person first.

Nurturing equanimity to build a caring culture requires the leadership team to recognize this link between personal growth and professional development. Doing so can have a positive impact on recruiting talent, engaging employees, and retaining workers over an extended period of time. Employees who do wish to develop professionally need to understand the corresponding necessity to grow personally as well.

Recent research by Korn Ferry stressed this link between professional development and personal growth when it noted, "69% of the world's most admired companies value learning agility and curiosity over career history and experience when it comes to hiring."[1] Learning agility refers to the dedication one has to a growth mindset in order to develop their personal traits while advancing their professional skill set. In a January 23, 2022 press release, the consulting firm McKinsey identified the following characteristics involved with traveling the path to personal and professional development: "developing new skills for continuous learning, seeking or providing mentorship, setting your leadership priorities, and

---

[1] K. Ferry. n.d. "Future of Work Trends in 2022: The New Era of Humanity." www.kornferry.com/insights/featured-topics/future-of-work/2022-future-of-work-trends.

taking care of your physical, mental, and emotional well-being."[2] Since professional growth involves learning new skills author Sarah Berry noted the linkage to personal development when she wrote "Personal development fits alongside professional growth so if you want to progress in your career, you'll need to develop personally first."[3]

Examples where professional development is linked to personal growth include the following scenarios and possibilities for those committed to growth in a caring culture:

- Taking on the responsibility for a larger budget than you currently do.
- Managing people or perhaps a larger team if you already manage others.
- Learning how to manage those who do not report into you.
- Attending professional training with a national organization.
- Volunteering with a local nonprofit in a supporting or leadership role.
- Assuming the leadership on an important project no one wanted due to its difficulty.
- Raising your profile by public speaking at a local, state, or national conference.

When the organizational culture fails to recognize how professional development is linked to personal growth and, thus, provides little to no incentives for employees to develop themselves, people leave or engage in quiet quitting. According to survey results published by Gallup on September 6, 2022 "Quiet quitters make up at least 50% of the U.S. workforce."[4] The definition of quiet quitting is quite simply when employees are doing the bare minimum to meet their job description. In the

---

[2] McKinsey press release. January 23, 2022. "Your Guide to Personal and Professional Development." www.mckinsey.com/featured-insights/themes/your-guide-to-personal-and-professional-development.

[3] S. Berry. April 11, 2018. "5 Ways to Manage Your Personal and Professional Development," *CV Library*. www.cv-library.co.uk/career-advice/development/5-ways-manage-professional-development/.

[4] J. Harter. September 6, 2022. "Is Quiet Quitting Real?" *Gallup*. www.gallup.com/workplace/398306/quiet-quitting-real.aspx.

organization lacks any demonstration of care toward its employees, quiet quitting could potentially get worse. Given the dynamics around work today, quiet quitting "is a problem because most jobs today require some level of extra effort to collaborate with coworkers and meet customer needs."[5] It is interesting to note that "before the pandemic, engagement and wellbeing were rising globally for nearly a decade; now in the post-COVID environment they are stagnant."[6] The reflection time provided to individuals helped them realize the three mantras of most global workers "Living for the weekend," "watching the clock tick," and "work is just a paycheck" they were longing for something more from their professional lives. In its 2022 State of the Global Workplace report, Gallup found "only 21% of employees engaged at work around the world." Additionally, 33% of employees reported an overall wellbeing of thriving. Sadly, most workers around the globe reported they do not find their work meaningful, do not think their lives are going well or do not feel hopeful about their future. Clearly, leaders have much more work to do to nurture equanimity and create a caring culture to reverse such findings and place workers in a positive trajectory both professionally and personally.[7]

New York City municipal workers provide just one example of a group of employees who are both disengaged and simply not putting up with an organizational culture that either lacks care or has an appearance that the environment fails to support its employees. In a July 13, 2022 article, *The New York Times* found that New York City's municipal workers' job vacancy rate was 7.7 percent as of March 2022, a startling five times higher when compared to recent years.[8] With so many New York City workers leaving, the city is experiencing difficulties delivering basic municipal services. "The wave of departures has included health care workers, parks employees, police officers and child protective service workers."[9] With better pay, more work-at-home

---

[5] Ibid.

[6] Gallup. n.d. "State of the Global Workplace: 2022 Report." www.gallup.com/workplace/349484/state-of-the-global-workplace-2022-report.aspx#ite-393245.

[7] Ibid.

[8] D. Rubinstein and E.G. Fitzsimmons. July 13, 2022. "Why City Workers in New York Are Quitting in Droves," *The New York Times*. www.nytimes.com/2022/07/13/nyregion/labor-shortage-nyc-jobs.html.

[9] Ibid.

schedules, and professional development growth opportunities in other organizations, New York City municipal workers merely exemplify what is going on around the United States in 2022. When organizational cultures fail to recognize the link between personal growth and professional development, and therefore lack the capacity to build a caring culture, employees leave or engage in quiet quitting. While this phenomenon existed prior to the pandemic, the post-COVID market has witnessed a substantial increase in the number of employees simply unwilling to tolerate the poor work cultures of yesterday.

As the consulting firm Korn Ferry noted in a 2022 report, the paradigm of power has shifted from organizations to people and from profit to mutual prosperity. In the post-COVID environment, more employees are searching for purpose and asking questions such as: Why am I doing this? What is it for? How can we do it better? As discussed earlier, millions of people are choosing to leave their jobs and, as a result, the competition to attract new talent is growing.[10] For those organizations that wish to remain vital, vibrant, and relevant, it will be imperative to nurture equanimity to build a caring culture. Failure to do so risks hiring, retaining, and recruiting the necessary human capital. When an organization faces a lack of human capital, it can experience an existential threat since an organization is only as good as the people it employs. As noted in the 2023 LinkedIn Workplace Learning Report "talent disruption, inflation, skills shortages, and global tension have followed pandemic tumult."[11] Therefore, organizations looking to create a sustainable future "will need to look beyond financial goals to consider the needs of employees, treat people as human beings, not parts of a machine, and ensure people feel connected to the company purpose and each other."[12]

---

[10] K. Ferry. n.d. "Future of Work Trends in 2022: The New Era of Humanity." www.kornferry.com/insights/featured-topics/future-of-work/2022-future-of-work-trends.

[11] LinkedIn Learning. n.d. *2023 Workplace Learning Report.* https://learning.linkedin.com/resources/workplace-learning-report.

[12] K. Ferry. n.d. "Future of Work Trends in 2022: The New Era of Humanity." www.kornferry.com/insights/featured-topics/future-of-work/2022-future-of-work-trends.

Perhaps the most important tool managers have in their armamentarium to help employees develop both personally and professionally is emotional intelligence (EI). EI refers to one's ability to recognize, understand, and manage their own emotions while simultaneously recognizing the emotions of others. When leaders develop their own EI, they are better positioned to manage teams, adapt their management style as needed, and utilize their emotions to influence positive outcomes more effectively.[13] Doing so will create an environment where individuals are provided opportunities to grow both personally and professionally. This need for EI at the intersection of personal and professional growth transcends industries, positions, and professions. Even a field as technical as architecture has recognized the need to leverage EI to grow personally and professionally.

As Dan Hart, 2022 American Institute of Architects President, said in an August 2, 2022 post, "Being an architect today requires technical acumen; emotional intelligence and empathy; professional integrity; the ability to envision and realize meaningful, positive change, and an overarching instinct and focus to bring it all together holistically."[14] To nurture equanimity and create a caring culture, leaders should embark upon a program of recognizing, developing, and enhancing EI of their people. By working on each of these attributes, managers can improve their overall EI to become better workplace leaders and build a caring culture.[15] Self-awareness, empathy, and resilience are three critical aspects of EI that leaders need to practice, and organizations need to support as doing so is instrumental to building a caring culture.

Self-awareness is a critical EI component since it allows one to better understand who they are and how they would like to intentionally respond

---

[13] HRDQ Staff. September 2, 2021. "The Importance of Emotional Intelligence in Leadership." https://hrdqstore.com/blogs/hrdq-blog/emotional-intelligence-leadership.

[14] D. Hart. August 2, 2022. "Relevancy and Impact: We Are the Change Agents We Seek," *AIA Architect.* www.architectmagazine.com/aia-architect/aiaperspective/relevancy-and-impact_o.

[15] HRDQ Staff. September 2, 2021. "The Importance of Emotional Intelligence in Leadership." https://hrdqstore.com/blogs/hrdq-blog/emotional-intelligence-leadership.

to a life situation. "With self-awareness, a person can make a conscious choice about behavior—they can scan the situation and identify the best behavioral choice."[16] During the pandemic, as people were locked down for weeks or even months at a time, they had the opportunity to ask such questions as "is it time to move to a new location or find a new job?"; "do I want to have my job define who I am?"; and "Do I want to continue to measure my self-worth by my level of productivity?"[17] Self-reflection during the pandemic allowed people to engage in the self-care required to admit that "the things that made them look 'successful' actually made them feel miserable, precarious, or physically unwell."[18] The daily grind in the prepandemic limited the amount of time people devoted to such questions. Perhaps another way of viewing that situation is during the prepandemic world, people did not set aside significant time to ponder life's huge questions. During the pandemic, however, "we've all had a year to evaluate if the life we're living is the one we want to be living," said Christina Wallace, a senior lecturer at Harvard Business School.[19] As Sarah Smalls from Vermont said, "It took a pandemic to come along and show me that you don't have a whole lot of time to do what you want to do. It gave me that nudge, and it was a hard nudge."[20]

Noting this behavioral change, Jennifer Levitz wrote in *The Wall Street Journal*, "the long pause that forced both isolation and introspection has been a catalyst to change course as people are emerging post-pandemic

---

[16] S. Haynie. April 27, 2021. "How Self-Awareness Takes Team Performance to New Heights in 2021," *ADT*. www.td.org/atd-blog/how-self-awareness-takes-team-performance-to-new-heights-in-2021.

[17] S. Samuel. June 9, 2020. "Quarantine Has Changed Us—and It's Not All Bad," *VOX*. www.vox.com/future-perfect/2020/6/9/21279258/coronavirus-pandemic-new-quarantine-habits.

[18] Ibid.

[19] K. Roose. April 21, 2021. "Welcome to the YOLO Economy," *The New York Times*. www.nytimes.com/2021/04/21/technology/welcome-to-the-yolo-economy.html.

[20] J. Levitz. April 11, 2021. "Covid-19 Was a Wake-Up Call, Leading Many to Make Lifestyle and Career Changes," *The Wall Street Journal*. www.wsj.com/articles/covid-19-was-a-wake-up-call-leading-many-to-make-lifestyle-and-career-changes-11618133400.

with new goals, priorities, and concerns."[21] As the pandemic crossed the year-long threshold, there evolved a growing amount of evidence that people were reassessing how they lived and worked.[22] A Pew Research Center survey published in February 2021 found 66 percent of unemployed people had "seriously considered" changing their field of work, a far greater percentage than during the 2007–2009 Great Recession.[23] People who used to work in restaurants or travel are finding higher-paying jobs in warehouses or real estate, for example. Technically, when workers take a while to figure out what new skills they need, or what jobs they might pivot to, is defined by economists as reallocation friction.[24]

Kevin Roose wrote about this reallocation friction in *The New York Times* on April 21, 2021 and noted "dozens of stories poured into my inboxes, all variations on the same basic theme of '*The pandemic changed my priorities, and I realized I didn't have to live like this.*'"[25] Further evidence of this new trend is the fact that "one-third of the of workers who switched jobs during the pandemic took a pay cut."[26] Layoffs, finding better work–life balance, and wanting to try something new were the top three reasons why people changed jobs or careers.[27] Such internal conversations are critical to practice self-awareness and increase one's EI post-COVID. In *The New York Times* opinion piece published May 13, 2020, StoryCorps founder Dave Isay commented on the amount of

---

[21] Ibid.

[22] H. Long. May 7, 2021. "It's Not a Labor Shortage," *The Washington Post*. www.washingtonpost.com/business/2021/05/07/jobs-report-labor-shortage-analysis/.

[23] R. Kochhar. March 18, 2021. "The Pandemic Stalls Growth in the Global Middle Class, Pushes Poverty Up Sharply," *Pew Research Center*. www.pewresearch.org/global/2021/03/18/the-pandemic-stalls-growth-in-the-global-middle-class-pushes-poverty-up-sharply/.

[24] H. Long. May 7, 2021. "It's Not a Labor Shortage," *The Washington Post*. www.washingtonpost.com/business/2021/05/07/jobs-report-labor-shortage-analysis/.

[25] K. Roose. April 21, 2021. "Welcome to the YOLO Economy," *The New York Times*. www.nytimes.com/2021/04/21/technology/welcome-to-the-yolo-economy.html.

[26] Prudential. February 2022. *The Pulse of the American Worker Survey*. https://news.prudential.com/presskits/pulse-american-worker-survey-entering-year-three-pandemic-american-workers-face-new-challenges-and-changes.htm.

[27] Ibid.

reflection time people had because of the pandemic and wrote "we have more time to reflect on the relationships that really matter in our lives" and proclaimed: "a conversation about life's big questions is the very definition of time well spent."[28]

Self-awareness is perhaps the most critical EI attribute for leaders of caring cultures to develop since it forms the foundation of a nurturing manager. A 2015 report titled "Stress in America: Paying with Our Health," published by the American Psychological Association (APA), emphasized just how important a manager's self-awareness plays in the culture of an organization. The APA reported "more than $500 billion is siphoned off from the U.S. economy because of workplace stress, and 550 million workdays are lost each year due to stress on the job." If you manage people, you have a direct impact on the amount of stress placed on employees. If you are unaware of this, now is the time to recognize this important role your position in management plays in the mental and physical health of others. If you are cognizant of this, then this serves as a reminder of just how important your management style is. In a December 2015 *Harvard Business Review* article, Emma Seppälä and Kim Cameron discussed the tremendous impact managers have on the health of those they manage and wrote "as a boss, you have a huge impact on how your employees feel."[29] Referencing a brain-imaging study, Seppälä and Cameron highlighted the fact that when "employees recalled a boss that had been unkind or un-empathic, they showed increased activation in areas of the brain associated with avoidance and negative emotion while the opposite was true when they recalled an empathic boss."[30]

One of the strategies effective managers use to demonstrate compassion toward those they manage is encouraging people to talk to them. This discussion can focus on problems at the office or personal issues. When your employees feel safe around you, when they trust you, and

---

[28] D. Isay. May 13, 2020. "Now Is the Time to Ask Your Loved Ones About Their Lives," *The New York Times*. www.nytimes.com/2020/05/13/opinion/quarantine-storycorps-interview.html.

[29] E. Seppälä and K. Cameron. December 1, 2015. "Proof That Positive Work Cultures Are More Productive," *Harvard Business Review*. https://hbr.org/2015/12/proof-that-positive-work-cultures-are-more-productive.

[30] Ibid.

when they know you have their best interests at heart, they will confide in you. As Seppälä and Cameron noted, "trusting that the leader has your best interests at heart improves employee performance." On the other hand, employee performance will most likely be negatively effective if employees lack trust in their manager or feel as though their manager is out to criticize them at every opportunity. Such an environment breeds little, if any, dialogue between manager and employees.

Recent research, however, suggests that compassion alone is not enough for effective management. In their December 2020 *Harvard Business Review* article, Rasmus Hougaard, Jacqueline Carter, and Nick Hobson wrote "Compassion on its own is not enough. For effective leadership, compassion must be combined with wisdom. By wisdom, we mean leadership competence, a deep understanding of what motivates people and how to manage them to deliver on agreed priorities."[31] To garner this wisdom, Hougaard and colleagues emphasized the need for managers to increase their self-awareness and self-compassion. As noted earlier, here is another reason why professional development is linked to personal growth. If a leader is going to demonstrate compassion for employees they must do so toward themselves first. "Self-compassion includes getting quality sleep and taking breaks during the day. For many leaders, self-compassion means letting go of obsessive self-criticism. Stop criticizing yourself for what you could have done differently or better."

In addition to self-awareness, empathy is another EI trait leaders of caring cultures should develop throughout their careers. Self-awareness was the first trait, and once a leader maintains an appropriate level, they can then work on enhancing the other EI attributes like empathy. American writer James Baldwin noted what connected humans across the globe when he wrote "You think your pain and your heartbreak are unprecedented in the history of the world, but then you read."[32]

---

[31] R. Hougaard, J. Carter, and N. Hobson. December 4, 2020. "Compassionate Leadership Is Necessary—but Not Sufficient," *Harvard Business Review.* https://hbr.org/2020/12/compassionate-leadership-is-necessary-but-not-sufficient.

[32] "You Think Your Pain and Your Heartbreak Are Unprecedented in the History of the World, But Then You Read." n.d. https://quoteinvestigator.com/2022/01/20/pain/#f+441077+1+1.

Books provided Baldwin a glimpse into the human experience around the world and taught him "that the things that tormented me most were the very things that connected me with all the people who were alive, who had ever been alive." If a leader is to nurture equanimity and build a caring culture, one must, in Baldwin's words "face the open wounds in themselves so can they understand them in other people." This connection, however, involves the three closely related, yet distinct, emotional attributes of empathy, sympathy, and compassion.

Empathy is defined as "the ability to understand and share the feelings of another" and is relatively new since it has been in circulation for the last 70 years or so. Common examples include empathizing with someone when they lose their job, experience the death of a loved one, or deal with the breakup of a romantic relationship. Do note, however, empathy can also involve happy occasions such as the announcement that a woman is pregnant, someone received a new job offer, or the engagement of a couple. Sympathy, however, has a different implication and stems from Latin *sympathia* meaning "community of feeling, sympathy." Sympathy involves recognizing, respecting, and acknowledging the feelings of others, not feeling another person's feelings, as is the case with empathy. One of the most common examples of an expression of sympathy is a message toward a friend when one of their loved ones dies. We extend sympathy messages to those we love when we want to acknowledge their feelings or experience. Compassion is action based and involves feeling the pain of someone else (empathy), recognizing the pain (sympathy), and then taking the steps, no matter how small, to help alleviate the pain (compassion). The literal interpretation of the word means compassion is "a suffering with another." Two examples of compassion are when you help someone arrange the funeral of a deceased loved one and when you bring food to a neighbor's home when they are sick.

All three characteristics help make up some of the many attributes of a caring culture. As Sam Tetrault wrote in a March 2020 blog post "empathy, sympathy, and compassion bring us closer as humans." Therefore, those leaders who wish to nurture equanimity can use these three, as well as other attributes, to create a culture forged in connections. According to author Scott Clark, the most important leadership skill to practice in 2022 is empathy as opposed to sympathy. When a business leader begins to emphasize empathy for the organization's employees, customers, and stakeholders, Clark believes doing so "provides them [leaders] with actionable insights that enhance products and services, as well as the lives of their customers and employees."[33] "Empathy goes deeper than sympathy in that it allows one to understand or share in the emotions or feelings that others experience as if they were personally put in a similar position," said Cheryl Brown Merriwether, vice president and executive director of ICARE, an Orlando, Florida-based center for addiction and recovery education.[34] In many organizations a lack of empathy exists and when that happens, misunderstandings, conflict, and division become the norm for that culture. For those leaders looking to nurture equanimity and build a caring culture, they need to, according to Merriwether, "openly and sincerely acknowledge and communicate the value and need for empathy within their teams, and look for ways to encourage, acknowledge and reinforce empathetic behaviors by others."[35] If done properly, the implementation of these empathetic behaviors can help the organization fill the void of trust and innovation, which, in turn, can help drive business growth and contribute to a more sustainable future.

To that point, Yong Kim described an empathetic leader as "someone who has honed the skill of recognizing the emotional needs of others and is able to use this skill to empower, support and understand their team."[36] Doing so is a critical component of nurturing equanimity and building a caring culture. When leaders instill empathy in the workplace, they can recognize when their employees are struggling and doing so demonstrates a high level of care. Leaders who routinely empower employees through difficult situations show they care and support the well-being of employees and in so doing, exemplify the work required to nurture equanimity and build a caring culture.[37]

---

[33] S. Clark. February 16, 2022. "The 2 Most Critical Leadership Skills of 2022." www.reworked.co/leadership/the-2-most-critical-leadership-skills-of-2022/.
[34] Ibid.
[35] Ibid.
[36] Y. King. June 21, 2022. "Why Empathy Is Key to Effective Leadership," *Forbes*. www.forbes.com/sites/forbesbusinesscouncil/2022/06/21/why-empathy-is-key-to-effective-leadership/?sh=16ae247766b6.
[37] Ibid.

According to APA, "resilience is the process and outcome of successfully adapting to difficult or challenging life experiences, especially through mental, emotional, and behavioral flexibility and adjustment to external and internal demands."[38] The ways in which individuals view and engage with the world, the availability and quality of social resources, and specific coping strategies are three of the many factors people have to adapt to adverse life situation. Psychological research demonstrates that the resources and skills associated with more positive adaptation (i.e., greater resilience) can be cultivated and practiced. With that in mind, leaders have the capacity to help their employees become more resilient should the organization choose to nurture equanimity and build a caring culture.

Organizations looking to build or enhance resilience have the ability to develop resilience training that teaches leaders—and eventually all employees—how to handle challenges and setbacks. Teresa Hopke, CEO of the Americas for global coaching firm Talking Talent, said there is a need for leaders to hone their human skills, including compassion, empathy, and vulnerability. For those leaders interested in creating a caring culture they should "learn how to slow down, pay attention to body language. pick up on nuances of conversations, check in with people after meetings and conversations to ensure they felt heard and were able to share."[39] Hopke said the best way to do so is through group or 1:1 coaching that seeks to identify mindsets and behaviors around their own leadership styles and approaches.

EI skills are the most valuable for those employees who are still feeling the stress of the pandemic. "Empathy, vulnerability, compassion—these are all things people are expecting their managers to show throughout the pandemic and beyond," she said.[40] Empathy and resilience are vital skills for both leaders and employees in the postpandemic world. Empathy allows people to gain a greater understanding of how others may feel

---

[38] Resilience as defined by the American Psychological Association. n.d. www.apa.org/topics/resilience/.

[39] S. Clark. February 16, 2022. "The 2 Most Critical Leadership Skills of 2022." www.reworked.co/leadership/the-2-most-critical-leadership-skills-of-2022/.

[40] Ibid.

and what they think, while resilience enables them to better deal with stress and anxiety in both the short and long term. "Leaders in all industries need to be empathetic, understanding and flexible with employees," HYPR's Simic said. "It's not only representative of good leadership but a healthy workplace as well."[41]

Building resilience, demonstrating empathy, and caring for employees encourages self-compassion among employees. Self-compassion has tremendous benefits, both physical and mental. For example, one study found that people who practice self-compassion have a lower risk of developing cardiovascular disease. The scientists found that those who scored higher on self-compassion had thinner carotid artery walls and less plaque buildup than those with lower self-compassion.[42] These indicators have been linked to a lower risk of heart attacks and strokes—years later. "These findings underscore the importance of practicing kindness and compassion, particularly towards yourself," said Dr. Rebecca Thurston, professor of psychiatry and psychology at the University of Pittsburgh. "We are all living through extraordinarily stressful times, and our research suggests that self-compassion is essential for both our mental and physical health."[43] Any leader looking to nurture equanimity and build a caring culture would certainly foster self-compassion among the organization's employees.

Leaders of organizations looking to nurture equanimity and build a caring culture recognize the various ways they can help support their employees to enhance the critical soft skill of resiliency. First, leaders can help employees identify, create, and enhance supportive networks. By allowing people to maintain healthy networks at work and home, an organization demonstrates to its employees the emphasis the culture places on nurturing relationships and positive connections. Providing a positive outlook is a second way leaders can help build resiliency among employees. By highlighting the options involved with a difficult situation,

---

[41] Ibid.

[42] "Women Who Practice Self-Compassion are at Lower Risk of Cardiovascular Disease." December 16, 2021. www.upmc.com/media/news/121621-thurston-self-compassion.

[43] Ibid.

leaders provide hope and help employees refocus away from the negative and toward the positive. Building resiliency among employees is a third option and provides an opportunity for the organization to teach people when to say no. Doing so sets clear boundaries and nurtures equanimity by helping to create more balance in an employee's work day.

A fourth lesson available to leaders wishing to promote resiliency among employees is the opportunity to help individuals understand what they can and cannot change. By teaching people the adage "focus on what you can do instead of what you cannot do," leaders can help manage expectations, communicate more clearly, and create a caring culture. Finally, a fifth lesson available to leaders looking to increase resiliency among employees is to demonstrate vulnerability. While leadership requires strength, confidence, and positivity, post-COVID organizations that will thrive require organizations to have leaders that understand and practice the fact that vulnerability is not a weakness, it's a strength. Resilience is a muscle, and by helping employees strengthen it, leaders and organizations can build happier, more stress-resistant teams and, in turn, nurture equanimity and build a caring culture.

Conclusion

This chapter illustrated the relationship between personal and professional growth and the role of three important soft skills: self-awareness, empathy, and resilience. These soft skills are also critical aspects of EI for those leaders and organizations concerned with nurturing equanimity and building a caring culture. The role of soft skills in the post-COVID market must be emphasized here as the research is overwhelmingly clear. For example, a report by the consulting firm Deloitte discovered that 92 percent of companies reported in a survey that "human capabilities or soft skills matter as much or more than hard skills in today's business world."[44] Soft skills include a wide range of capabilities including oral

---

[44] B. Robinson. August 1, 2022. "3 Soft Skills Required to Complete in Today's Post-Pandemic Workplace," *Forbes*. www.forbes.com/sites/bryanrobinson/2022/08/01/3-soft-skills-required-to-compete-in-todays-post-pandemic-workplace/?sh=845973d37278.

and written communication, small group and large group collaboration, adaptability and problem-solving and are often considered fundamental to effective teamwork and organizational success. While the continued emphasis on soft skills will continue into the foreseeable future, those organizations creating a caring culture will also recognize the link between personal and professional growth as they work toward the next step in the process of creating a caring culture and that is defining and nurturing equanimity.

CHAPTER 4

Defining Equanimity

For those organizations dedicated to nurturing equanimity and building a caring culture, Chapters 1 and 2 examined the market realities and strategic imperatives relevant in today's post-COVID marketplace. Chapter 3 then detailed the link between personal and professional growth that leaders should use as a focus point as they build a caring culture. In this chapter, the attention now shifts to equanimity itself to help managers and leaders better understand how important this aspect of culture is for organizations. Traditionally, equanimity is defined as a deeply profound, dynamic, and beautiful state of mind applicable to almost any life situation.[1] As Susan M. Pollak wrote in a 2017 *Psychology Today* article "Equanimity is an essential practice for our troubled and chaotic times."[2]

In today's post-COVID volatile, uncertain, complex, and ambiguous global marketplace, wisdom is needed now more than ever to help organizations succeed. To increase their self-awareness leaders would serve themselves and their organizations well by recalling the observation meditation teacher Sharon Salzberg made when she called equanimity the 'secret ingredient' in mindfulness as it leads to wisdom. Pollak noted that equanimity allows one to meet every personal and professional life situation "with an open and responsive heart."[3] For those leaders looking to either find balance in their own lives, or help their employees find balance in their own life situations, equanimity serves as a tremendously useful approach. As Pollack summarized, equanimity provides one with

---

[1] A. Murphy. 2017. "The Ten Kinds of Equanimity (Upekkha)," *Journal of Social Sciences and Humanities* II, no. 2.

[2] S.M. Pollak. October 4, 2017. "Equanimity: A Practice for Troubled Times," *Psychology Today*. www.psychologytoday.com/us/blog/the-art-now/201710/equanimity-practice-troubled-times.

[3] Ibid.

the opportunity to "not get overwhelmed and to meet challenging events without being shattered. It is a steadiness of mind and a calm understanding that allows us to be with the constantly changing and shifting landscape of our world."[4]

To rephrase the traditional definition and make it applicable to the post-COVID workplace culture, equanimity, as used throughout this chapter and the entire publication, is defined as an even-minded mental state or dispositional tendency toward all experiences or objects, regardless of their affective valence (pleasant, unpleasant, or neutral) or source. The term even-mindedness is synonymous with the common definition of equanimity as a state of being calm, stable, and composed. Equanimity also involves a level of impartiality (i.e., being not partial or biased), such that one can experience unpleasant thoughts or emotions without repressing, denying, judging, or having an aversion for them.[5]

Similarly, in a state of equanimity, one can have pleasant or rewarding experiences without becoming overexcited (e.g., to the point of mania or hypomania), trying to prolong these experiences, or becoming addicted to them. In addition, it should be noted that the ideal form of equanimity embraced by Buddhism also includes having an equal attitude toward all beings, without the boundaries that we habitually draw between friends, strangers, and those we consider "difficult people"; in other words, "regarding all beings as equal in their right to have happiness and avoid suffering" and "treating them free from discrimination, without preferences and prejudices."[6] For those leaders and managers dedicated to build a caring culture, this chapter examines three elements of equanimity: moderation, regulation, and cultivation. Understanding each one, its role, and how to incorporate each element into the organization's core values is essential to nurturing equanimity and building a caring culture.

---

[4] Ibid.

[5] G. Desbordes, T. Gard, E.A. Hoge, B.K. Hölzel, C. Kerr, S.W. Lazar, A. Olendzki, and D.R. Vago. April 2015. "Moving Beyond Mindfulness: Defining Equanimity as an Outcome Measure in Meditation and Contemplative Research," *Mindfulness* (New York, NY), 6, no. 2, pp. 356–372. www.ncbi.nlm .nih.gov/pmc/articles/PMC4350240/.

[6] Ibid.

Moderation

Brad Cousins discussed the significance of equanimity in business culture in his *Forbes* article "Finding the True 'E' of Entrepreneurship: Equanimity."[7] Since stress is omnipresent in most organizations as the world continues to figure out a way forward through the ambiguity of a post-COVID marketplace, Cousins noted that "entrepreneurs, innovators and leaders in crisis all require a level of equanimity in order to maintain resilience."[8] One strategy leaders have to practice equanimity and maintain resilience amidst a crisis of any proportion is known as the Golden Mean. The Golden Mean is defined as the desirable middle between two extremes, one of excess and the other of deficiency. Irish writers Oscar Wilde and Flann O'Brien provide two observations on this point. Wilde observed, "Everything in moderation, including moderation," while Flann O'Brien noted, "Moderation, we find, is an extremely difficult thing to get in this country." Moderation is synonymous with the Golden Mean.

The Golden Mean appeared in Greek thought at least as early as the Delphic maxims "nothing in excess" and was emphasized in later Aristotelian philosophy. For example, in the Aristotelian view, courage is a virtue, but if taken to excess would manifest as recklessness and, in deficiency, cowardice. Being agile, disciplined, and intentional will allow one to know when to pursue the Golden Mean and when to use an extreme. Pursuing the Golden Mean affords one the flexibility required to answer questions, resolve issues, and address problems as they arise while dealing with one organizational issue after another. Oscillating from one extreme to the next, all the while keeping the Golden Mean in site, can be a powerful strategy to use while creating a caring culture coupled with remaining relevant. Pursuing the Golden Mean provides one with the focus required to understand the extremes and the difference between abusing them and using them appropriately.

---

[7] B. Cousins. September 23, 2021. "Find the True 'E' of Entrepreneurship: Equanimity," *Forbes*. www.forbes.com/sites/forbescoachescouncil/2021/09/23/finding-the-true-e-of-entrepreneurship-equanimity/?sh=2b9a583014e8.

[8] Ibid.

The adjacent table provides the Golden Mean associated with 10 characteristics often associated with leaders as well as their related deficiencies and excesses.

Left Extreme	Balance	Right Extreme
Deficiency (–)	Golden Mean	Excess (+)
Cowardice	Courage	Rashness
Stinginess	Generosity	Extravagance
Sloth	Ambition	Greed
Humility	Modesty	Pride
Secrecy	Honesty	Loquacity
Moroseness	Humor	Absurdity
Quarrelsomeness	Friendship	Flattery
Self-indulgence	Temperance	Insensibility
Apathy	Composure	Irritability
Indecisiveness	Self-control	Impulsiveness

To illustrate the Golden Mean, the example of a coward is a good reference point. During an organizational crisis, when one fails to speak up, act, or attempt to resolve the situation, they are demonstrating the characteristics of a coward. On the other hand, during a crisis, when one uses reckless abandon to speak up, act, or resolve the situation, they are on the opposite end of the spectrum. The Golden Mean between being a coward and reckless abandon is courage. A courageous person is neither a coward nor a reckless abandon. This person, according to Aristotle, would be living a virtuous life. A person demonstrating such courage would be balanced in their approach to a specific life situation, having discovered the Golden Mean. Nurturing equanimity and building a caring culture by pursuing the Golden Mean is no easy task as it requires a high degree of self-awareness, strict discipline, and attention to detail.

A modern reference to the Golden Mean can be found in Megan Garber's July/August 2021 article "Top Gun Is an Infomercial for America," published in *The Atlantic*. Reflecting upon the 35th anniversary of the film's release, Garber wrote:

To watch Top Gun now, freshly aware of how easily rugged individualism can take a turn toward the toxic, is to appreciate anew the film's dicey feat: For its redemption story to land, its hero must be arrogant but not malignant, culpable but capable, infuriating but also easy to love. Maverick's is a load-bearing charm. And his film's willingness to pamper him raises still-fraught questions about selfish entitlement. Who gets the gift of multiple second chances, and who does not? Who has to follow the rules? Who is allowed to break them?

Answering these and other questions can help one understand the moderation trait of equanimity; it is also important to consider the role regulation plays in achieving a state of balance in a culture that cares.

In their 2017 book *Peak Performance: Elevate Your Game, Avoid Burnout, and Thrive with the New Science of Success*, authors Brad Stulberg and Steve Magness emphasized the need for rest, especially for athletes and devised the equation *Stress + Rest = Growth*. This simple formula compliments the moderation of equanimity and is central to the achievement of balance in one's life. Stulberg and Magness acknowledged it is

as simple and as hard as that. As an athlete, if you want to improve something—your 100-meter time, say, or your deadlift personal record—you've got to apply a challenge, some sort of stressor and then follow it with a period of rest and recovery. Too much stress without enough rest and you get injury, illness, and burnout. Not enough stress plus too much rest and you get complacency, boredom, and stagnation.

They based their equation on research conducted by the American College of Sports Medicine, the country's premier body on the application of fitness science, that officially endorsed training in this manner to increase size and strength. Meanwhile, a 2015 study published in the journal *Frontiers in Physiology* found that the best endurance athletes in the world all have one thing in common: They oscillate between periods of stress and rest.

This equation of *Stress + Rest = Growth* can be found elsewhere and applied to other aspects of life, notably work. For example, Researcher Alex Soojung-Kim Pang published his results in a March 2017 article titled "Darwin Was a Slacker and You Should Be Too," in which he declares, "Many famous scientists have something in common—they didn't work long hours. In fact, some of the greatest geniuses 'worked' only four hours a day."[9] How is that possible? How can the world's greatest minds only work for a few hours each day? Well, the short answer is they rested. Specifically, the scientists rested in-between bouts of creative transformation, generally operating in bursts of productivity lasting between 90 and 120 minutes. Implicitly they recognized what science now demonstrates—that the body as an information system always rebuilds and renews. Humans, in other words, need downtime to recharge and regulate their energy levels. In human downtime, the body is continually learning, especially when asleep. Rest is not only necessary for life and survival but also for the creative capacities that will power knowledge industries of the future. Biological intelligence can do more than make individuals smarter; it can enhance the performance of communities and societies. Here are just a few examples:

- Charles Darwin split his day into morning and evening work, doing about four hours total.
- G.H. Hardy, one of the greatest mathematicians of the 20th century and author of a celebrated autobiography, worked in a four-hour stint in the morning but with breaks.
- The great novelist Anthony Trollope wrote his 2,500 words a day between 5:30 and 8:30 a.m. before rushing off to help run the British Postal Service; to him, we also owe a version of the postbox.

According to Alex Soojung-Kim Pang, scientists who spent 25 hours in the workplace were no more productive than those who spent five. The 60-plus-hour-a-week researchers were the least productive of all. The best students generally followed a pattern of practicing hardest and

---

[9] "Q&A: with Alex Soojung-Kim Pang." November 1, 2016. *Scientific American*. www.scientificamerican.com/article/q-a-with-alex-soojung-kim-pang/.

longest in the morning, taking a nap in the afternoon, and then having a second practice.[10]

In other words, *Stress + Rest = Growth*. Interestingly enough, this equation has been around for centuries and periodically emerges from the work or artists. For example, poet Maya Angelou once wrote:

> Every person needs to take one day away. A day in which one consciously separates the past from the future. Jobs, family, employers, and friends can exist one day without any one of us, and if our egos permit us to confess, they could exist eternally in our absence. Each person deserves a day away in which no problems are confronted, no solutions searched for. Each of us needs to withdraw from the cares which will not withdraw from us.

To that end, organizations have started to implement new policies post-COVID to help cultivate a caring culture where individuals have opportunities to "withdraw from their cares," recharge, and reengage.

When an organization shifts its attention to the third component of equanimity, it does so with the intention of cultivating an environment where people can work toward balance in order to recharge and reengage. Organizational culture is often assessed on two separate yet related variables: alignment (when employees know the culture and believe it is appropriate for the organization) and connectedness (when they identify with and support the culture). Together, these two measures— culture alignment and culture connectedness—are key to assuring culture impact. The COVID-19 pandemic provided an unavoidable opportunity for organizations to assess the process by which they cultivated organizational culture as well as its impact on employee engagement. Leaders and managers have started to learn just how antiquated their pre-COVID approaches to culture were. For example, for those managers interested in creating a caring environment, they have realized that having employees working in the same building does not in and of itself create a healthy company culture. Nor is company culture created by a one-time

---

[10] Ibid.

statement of leadership's vision. COVID global pandemic made leaders across organizations, sectors, and industries understand that cultivating a caring culture requires an ongoing, conscious, and deliberate effort. It is created over time and must be cultivated.[11] With a December 2021 Gartner survey of more than 3,900 hybrid/remote knowledge workers revealing only one in four employees are connected to their organization's culture, it would appear that much more work needs to be done when it comes to nurturing equanimity and creating a caring culture.[12]

This lack of connectedness to culture, as reported in December 2021, did not happen overnight and started well before the pandemic. Prior to COVID, leaders and managers across all types of organizations spent a disproportionate amount of time on cultivating culture as they invested heavily on alignment and little on connectedness. "Historically, senior leaders have intentionally invested in driving culture alignment, but have primarily relied on culture connectedness to occur through 'osmosis:' relying on time in offices, in-person and at a macroscale to make employees feel connected to culture," said Cambon. "Employees at all levels, and across demographics, are suffering from a connectedness crisis, which suggests this problem isn't just related to hybrid and remote work, but to organizations' lack of intentionality in driving connectedness historically."[13] "Hybrid and remote work hasn't necessarily changed our culture, it's changed the way we experience culture," said Alexia Cambon, director in the Gartner HR practice.

> While employers used to be able to frame their cultural values and hang them on the walls for employees to see, this no longer works today when hybrid and remote knowledge workers spend 65% less time in offices than before the pandemic.[14]

---

[11] Edison Partners. December 16, 2020. "Cultivating Culture: Why and How to Improve Organizational Culture." www.edisonpartners.com/blog/cultivating-culture.

[12] "Gartner Says HR Leaders Are Struggling to Adapt Current Organizational Culture to Support a Hybrid Workforce." May 17, 2022. www.gartner.com/en/newsroom/press-releases/2022-05-17-gartner-says-hr-leaders-are-struggling-to-adapt-current-organizational-culture-to-support-a-hybrid-workforce.

[13] Ibid.

[14] Ibid.

One such organization that has started to think differently about how it cultivates organizational culture is Bucknell University. In his August 2022 University Address, Bucknell President John Bravman identified one of his top priorities is for Bucknell to become a premier employer in the region. Bucknell University is a private liberal arts college in Lewisburg, Pennsylvania, with over 3,000 students and 1,300 employees. On October 25, 2022, Bravman took a significant step forward to achieving that goal when he informed employees that the University Thanksgiving break this year will include Monday, November 21 and Tuesday, November 22, in addition to the traditional closing of University offices on Wednesday, Thursday, and Friday, November 23 through 25—giving all employees a full week off. "This pilot program, recommended in collaboration with the Office of Human Resources, recognizes the importance of mental health and wellness, allowing us to enjoy more time with family and return to our campus duties refreshed and recharged," Bravman wrote in his e-mail to employees.[15] This additional time off followed a previous announcement when Bravman informed employees that Bucknell offices will annually close for two weeks for the holiday break during the final two weeks of December through New Year's Day. According to Bravman, the week off at Thanksgiving and then two weeks off at the end of December are two attempts to "strengthen our benefits package, further distinguish Bucknell from other area employers, and help us attract and retain the most talented professionals in an increasingly competitive market."[16] Bucknell's new model in the post-COVID work environment exemplifies the regulation aspect of an organization that nurtures equanimity and creates a caring culture.

Conclusion

For those leaders and managers dedicated to build a caring culture, this chapter examined three elements of equanimity: moderation, regulation, and cultivation. Understanding each one, its role, and how to incorporate

[15] B. Simpson. November 11, 2022. "Bucknell increases employee benefits for Thanksgiving Break," *The Bucknellian.* https://bucknellian.net/114351/news/bucknell-increases-employee-benefits-for-thanksgiving-break/.
[16] Ibid.

each element into the organization's core values is essential to nurturing equanimity and building a caring culture. To be effective at their job in the post-COVID global marketplace, 76 percent of employees reported that culture was extremely important. Additionally, 61 percent of human resource leaders say that to achieve organizational goals, culture is more important in a hybrid work model than in an on-site work model.[17] Moreover, 66 percent of executives believe that culture is more important than an organization's business strategy or operating model. The rise of remote and hybrid work has had a significant impact on the way individuals work in the post-COVID environment. Recent research shows 65 percent of employees have reported that their company culture has changed since the COVID-19 pandemic. As workplaces have changed, so too has the organizational culture.

Some leaders and managers have figured out how to nurture equanimity and create a caring culture, while most have yet to do so. Those organizations that have adapted their approach to culture have figured out how to create an attractive value proposition for prospective talent, keep current employees engaged amidst periods of significant change, and demonstrate greater flexibility with work-from-home policies. Other organizations, however, especially those slow to evolve in the post-COVID environment, focused their energy on "getting back to normal" and instead have had to deal with the consequences of disengagement, burnout, and unwanted turnover among employees. Recent research shows disengaged employees are 3.8 times more likely than their engaged counterparts to cite organizational culture as a reason for leaving.[18] Since "employees criticize their corporate cultures for hundreds of flaws—including risk aversion, excess bureaucracy, insularity, and an impersonal feel, to mention just a few,"

---

[17] "Gartner Says HR Leaders Are Struggling to Adapt Current Organizational Culture to Support a Hybrid Workforce." May 17, 2022. www.gartner.com/en/newsroom/press-releases/2022-05-17-gartner-says-hr-leaders-are-struggling-to-adapt-current-organizational-culture-to-support-a-hybrid-workforce.
[18] Quantum Workplace: 2022 Organizational Culture Research Report. 2022. https://marketing.quantumworkplace.com/hubfs/Marketing/Research/2022%20Organizational%20Culture%20Research%20Report.pdf.

it is no surprise that a lack of clarity around the definition of culture varies among leaders and managers.[19]

What is clear, however, is that culture starts at the top, Leaders and managers have a responsibility to define the organizational culture clearly. Once defined, leaders and managers then need to implement the three elements of equanimity: moderation, regulation, and cultivation throughout the organization. Doing so can help foster what the level of support for self-care individuals are searching for from employers in the post-COVID environment.

---

[19] Donald Sull, Charles Sull, William Cipolli, and Caio Brighenti, "Why Every Leader Needs to Worry About Toxic Culture," *MIT Sloan Management Review,* March 16, 2022. https://sloanreview.mit.edu/article/why-every-leader-needs-to-worry-about-toxic-culture/

CHAPTER 5

Prioritizing Self-Care

As people around the globe learned to deal with the emotional, social, economic, and physical ripple effects of the COVID-19 global pandemic, they engaged in self-care to manage their personal and professional development during such a stressful time. As a result of this increased awareness of how essential self-care is to practice, leaders and managers started to treat it with the priority self-care deserves. As Jacqueline Ashley noted in *Forbes*, "even though leaders in some organizations may recognize self-care is important, it's not always treated with the priority it deserves."[1] The emergence of self-care as a prioritization for both the employer and employee has been a positive development in the last two years as the world continues to emerge post-COVID. Much work still needs to be done. Sadly, it took a global pandemic for individuals and organizations to realize the critical role self-care plays on both the personal and professional levels. Two groups in particular, front-line health care workers and educators, faced tremendous challenges to overcome and in so doing learned firsthand the value of prioritizing self-care during the pandemic.

Since frontline workers never had the opportunity to work from home, like so many people were forced to do during the global shutdown, they dealt with COVID-19 upfront and personal, unlike so many other workers. Nurses, emergency medical technicians, paramedics, physicians, office staff, and other health care workers even jeopardized their own health at times to help save patients. While many first responders clearly understood what life was like on the front lines, the majority of people

---

[1] J. Ashley. June 28, 2021. "Why Multidimensional Self-Care Is Essential to Better Leadership," *Forbes*. www.forbes.com/sites/forbescoachescouncil/2021/06/28/why-multidimensional-self-care-is-essential-to-better-leadership/?sh=77f6e8425d56.

failed to realize the challenges posed by COVID. For example, Mary Turner, a registered nurse in Minneapolis was unable to comfort her own father as he lay dying alone of COVID in a nurse home. As Turner noted "People don't realize what it was like to be on the front lines and risking your own safety without adequate protective gear while dealing with so much death."[2]

Further evidence of the stress experienced by front-line health care workers during the pandemic came from an October poll of 862 emergency physicians nationwide from the American College of Emergency Physicians and Morning Consult that found 87 percent felt more stressed since the onset of COVID-19, with 72 percent experiencing a greater degree of professional burnout.[3] A November 15, 2022 press release published by the American Educational Research Association reported the results of a study of educators across the United States and found that "U.S. teachers were 40 percent more likely to report anxiety symptoms than healthcare workers, 20 percent more likely than office workers, and 30 percent more likely than workers in other occupations, such as military, farming, and legal professions."[4]

Such mental health concerns continued as some schools struggled creating a balance of in-person and remote classes. reopened and teachers returned in person. For example, "teachers who taught remotely were 60 percent more likely to report feelings of isolation than their in-person peers."[5] The need to prioritize self-care was evident well before the pandemic since "teacher well-being was a major concern for school leaders."[6] Additionally, a Rand Corporation survey found that twice as

[2] A. Jacobs. August 26, 2021. "Frontline Health Care Workers Aren't Feeling the 'Summer of Joy'," *The New York Times*. www.nytimes.com/2021/07/01/health/covid-nurses-doctors-burnout.html.

[3] "Poll: Workplace Stigma, Fear of Professional Consequences Prevent Emergency Physicians from Seeking Mental Health Care." n.d. www.emergencyphysicians.org/mentalhealthpoll.

[4] "Study: Teachers Experienced More Anxiety Than Healthcare Workers During the Pandemic, press release." November 15, 2022. American Educational Research Association. www.aera.net/Newsroom/Study-Teachers-Experienced-More-Anxiety-than-Healthcare-Workers-During-the-Pandemic.

[5] Ibid.

[6] Ibid.

many principals and teachers reported frequent job-related stress as other working adults.[7] Fortunately, individuals across the professional spectrum realized, or perhaps were made to realize, the significance of prioritizing self-care.

Dr. Michelle Thompson, chair of medicine for the University of Pittsburgh Medical Center Horizon regional health service, was seeing about 25 patients a day in her office when the pandemic forced a shutdown. To continue helping her patients, Dr. Thompson converted to telemedicine but doing so took a toll on her mental health. Recognizing the need for self-care during such a chaotic time, Dr. Thompson joined an eight-week online mind-body skills program run by Dr. James S. Gordon, founder and executive director of The Center for Mind-Body Medicine. The program and related support group helped her understand the value of prioritizing her self-care routine as she would check in with herself to ask such questions as "What do I need? How am I caring for myself in this moment? Do I need a cup of tea? Should I implement some mind-body medicine?"[8] Accepting that the pandemic proved to be "the hardest time of her life," Dr. Thompson spoke to her ability to nurture her own equanimity when she said "I am super grounded and really well balanced. I am doing OK, but it is constant work and making sure I'm staying aware of my own self."[9]

Just as Dr. Thompson switched to remote health care via telemedicine, so too did educators across the globe. Teaching, especially at the K-12 level was exhausting on a good day prior to the pandemic. During COVID, however, and as schools were mandated to hold remote learning, teaching quickly became exhausting on the emotional, intellectual, and physical levels. According to high school science teacher Veronica Wylie, "prior to the pandemic, I worked until I had nothing left of myself

---

[7] M. Casey. August 27, 2022. "School Districts Move to Ease Teacher Stress, Burnout: 'The Pandemic Was So Hard and So Impactful and So Stressful,'" *Fortune.* https://fortune.com/2022/08/27/school-districts-ease-teacher-stress-burnout-coronavirus-covid-pandemic/.

[8] A. Ellin. January 26, 2021. "Doctors, Facing Burnout, Turn to Self-Care," *The New York Times.* www.nytimes.com/2021/01/26/well/mind/doctors-facing-burnout-turn-to-self-care.html.

[9] Ibid.

to give" referring to creating endless lesson plans, grading countless assignments, and completing one administrative task after another. In an editorial detailing, her experience and awakening on the importance of self-care, Wylie noted, "during the pandemic I learned that life is too short to waste it pretending that I can be all things to all people at all times; that self-care is not selfish; that it is a necessity, not a luxury."[10]

Coinciding with such an awakening at the individual level was the emergence of self-care at the organizational level. Organizations large and small, private and public, and across different industries started to nurture equanimity to create a caring culture that prioritized self-care. As LinkedIn noted in its *2022 Global Trends Report* "company culture is having a watershed moment as it is being reshaped in a crucible fired by the pandemic, the acceleration of automation, the rise of millennials and Gen Z in the workforce, and the Great Reshuffle."[11] As a result of these dynamics shaping the COVID and post-COVID workplace "employees are demanding—and quite often getting—more freedom to work where and when they want and more attention to their well-being."[12]

As a result, the post-COVID workplace looks very different than it did before the pandemic and continues to evolve as organizations navigate the dynamics of today's hypercompetitive, ever-changing, and ambiguous economy. During the pandemic, many organizations were forced to either close or adjust how they approached the mental, physical, and emotional well-being of their employees. According to the American Psychological Association (APA), "facing the stress of isolation, fears of the virus, and an overwhelming news cycle, it appears many workplace leaders have realized the need to address mental health concerns among

---

[10] V. Wylie. December 31, 2021. "A New Mindset for Teachers: Self-Care Is Not Selfish," EdSurge. www.edsurge.com/news/2021-12-31-a-new-mindset-for-teachers-self-care-is-not-selfish.

[11] LinkedIn. n.d. "2022 Global Talent Trends: The Reinvention of Company Culture." https://business.linkedin.com/content/dam/me/business/en-us/talent-solutions-lodestone/body/pdf/global_talent_trends_2022.pdf.

[12] LinkedIn. n.d. "2022 Global Talent Trends: The Reinvention of Company Culture." https://business.linkedin.com/content/dam/me/business/en-us/talent-solutions-lodestone/body/pdf/global_talent_trends_2022.pdf.

their staff."[13] The results of APA's *2022 Work and Well-being Survey* reveal that 7 in 10 workers (71 percent) believe their employer is more concerned about the mental health of employees now than in the past. This new focus is highly valued by employees with 81 percent of individuals reporting looking for work cultures that support mental health when they seek future job opportunities.[14] The prioritization of self-care is a new dynamic that leaders and managers need to address if they would like to nurture equanimity and create a caring culture. For those employers struggling with recruitment and retention, one strategy they can employ is to engage employees to take charge of their own well-being. Doing so can help the organization differentiate itself from others as the battle for top talent and human capital continues.[15]

Additional research conducted by the consulting firm WTW (formerly Willis Towers Watson) echoed the APA findings and found three significant developments[16]:

- 86 percent of employers said mental health, stress, and burnout were still a priority.
- 49 percent, however, had not formally articulated a well-being strategy for their workforce.
- 26 percent had adopted a well-being strategy.

"As stress and burnout levels continue to climb amid the ongoing pandemic, employers are putting the overall well-being of their employees at the top of their list," said Regina Ihrke, WTW's senior director, health, and benefits. "The organizations that most effectively move the needle are those that develop a comprehensive strategy that supports all aspects

---

[13] "Workers Appreciate and Seek Mental Health Support in the Workplace." n.d. American Psychological Association. www.apa.org/pubs/reports/work-well-being/2022-mental-health-support.
[14] Ibid.
[15] S. Miller. January 26, 2022. "Employers Identify Workforce Mental Health Priorities for 2022," SHRM. www.shrm.org/resourcesandtools/hr-topics/benefits/pages/employers-identify-workforce-mental-health-priorities-for-2022.aspx.
[16] W.T. Watson. n.d. *Wellbeing Diagnostic.* www.wtwco.com/en-US/Solutions/products/wellbeing-diagnostic.

of their employees' well-being. It's also important to articulate that strategy to employees, conduct manager training and measure effectiveness."[17] As Kristin Lee wrote in *Psychology Today*, organizations need to "bake mental health support into work cultures." To nurture equanimity and build a caring culture, baking mental health support into the employee experience means providing time paid time off, creating flexible work conditions, and treating people like actual human beings. "Work cultures that strive to avoid punitive and hierarchical ways, and instead work to build psychological safety and trust can breed the conditions that help mitigate burnout."[18] After helping leaders incorporate self-care into work cultures, Amy Jen Su echoed similar sentiment and observed "One CEO I worked with summed it up best when he said: 'Self-care is no longer a luxury; it's part of the job.'"[19]

One model available to leaders and managers in those organizations who wish to nurture equanimity and create a caring culture by prioritizing self-care is the Substance Abuse and Mental Health Services Administration's (SAMHSA) Wellness Initiative. Since self-care and wellness is a broad concept, the SAMHSA provides individuals with a multidimensional approach for consideration that involves eight different elements: emotional, physical, occupational, intellectual, financial, social, environmental, and spiritual. "These dimensions are interconnected, one dimension building on another."[20] By using this model, leaders and managers can prioritize self-care within a framework that covers eight different aspects of an individual's life. Such comprehensive coverage of

---

[17] S. Miller. January 26, 2022. "Employers Identify Workforce Mental Health Priorities for 2022," SHRM. www.shrm.org/resourcesandtools/hr-topics/benefits/pages/employers-identify-workforce-mental-health-priorities-for-2022.aspx.

[18] K. Lee. June 1, 2022. "We Can't 'Self-Care' Our Way Out of Our Mental Health Crisis," *Psychology Today*. www.psychologytoday.com/us/blog/rethink-your-way-the-good-life/202206/we-can-t-self-care-our-way-out-our-mental-health-crisis.

[19] A.J. Su. June 19, 2017. "6 Ways to Weave Self-Care Into Your Workday," *Harvard Business Review*. https://hbr.org/2017/06/6-ways-to-weave-self-care-into-your-workday.

[20] The Substance Abuse and Mental Health Services Administration. n.d. "Creating a Healthier Life: A Step-by-Step Guide to Wellness." https://store.samhsa.gov/sites/default/files/d7/priv/sma16-4958.pdf.

self-care demonstrates a high level of commitment the organization has toward its employees. For SAMHSA, "wellness is about how we live our lives and the joy and fulfillment and health we experience."[21] To help leaders and managers better understand the interconnectedness of these eight elements of self-care and wellness, here is an example to consider as the organization looks to nurture equanimity and create a caring culture.

When employees worry about money (most recently the escalating price of consumer goods outpacing pay raises), individuals may experience anxiety (emotional). With anxiety comes the possibility of related medical problems (physical) and even the potential for negative experiences at work (occupational). When this happens, the employee may start to question their sense of meaning and purpose (spiritual). Additionally, if an employee is laid off due to the financial collapse of their organization, and therefore, through no fault of their own, they stop working (occupational), lose opportunities to interact with others who they worked so closely with for years (social), and may not be able to afford the good food and medical care they need to stay well (physical). If the situation gets critical, the employee may even need to move out of their residence and into a more affordable place that feels less safe and secure (environmental). The SAMHSA model of self-care and wellness is one of many available to leaders and managers.

It is important to note the repercussions of failing to build a caring culture in general and prioritizing self-care specifically. According to studies pre and post COVID, 20 percent of employees left a job at some point in their career because of its toxic culture.[22] Companies with a toxic culture will lose employees, struggle to replace workers who leave, and need to manage negative online reviews of their toxic work cultures. Having a toxic employer brand makes it harder to attract candidates. The important takeaway from this chapter is that the prioritization of self-care, and its multidimensional elements, should remain a priority in

---

[21] The Substance Abuse and Mental Health Services Administration. n.d. "Creating a Healthier Life: A Step-by-Step Guide to Wellness." https://store .samhsa.gov/sites/default/files/d7/priv/sma16-4958.pdf.
[22] D. Sull, C. Sull, W. Cipolli, and C. Brighenti. March 16, 2022. "Why Every Leader Needs to Worry About Toxic Culture," *MIT Sloan Management Review*. https://sloanreview.mit.edu/article/why-every-leader-needs-to-worry-about-toxic-culture/.

2023 and beyond for any organization looking to create a caring culture, retain workers, and attract new employees.

Conclusion

The COVID-19 global pandemic changed work forever. Those clamoring to go back to "business as usual" know that such thinking is outdated and, one could argue, things were never "normal" in the first place. One thing is certain, however, and that is "work will be less about place and more about people's potential."[23] One of the byproducts of this prioritization of self-care and wellness that emerged during COVID is that the majority of employees in office-based positions would like the ability to work from home as part of their employment agreement. According to a 2021 Accenture survey, "83% of workers said a hybrid model would be optimal."[24] An organizational culture that supports a hybrid work environment prioritizes self-care and wellness. But not every organization can offer its workers hybrid as a perk. The future of work in 2023 and in the immediate future will be characterized by complexity and managing differences in a volatile, uncertain, complex, and ambiguous world. Organizations will simply struggle to provide working models that satisfy the needs of all workers, all the time.[25] Thus, leaders and managers need to be agile in their thinking, open to new ideas, and willing to challenge assumptions in order to create a caring environment. Organizations that continue to place employee well-being and experience at the forefront of their decisions will remain relevant and have a competitive advantage beyond the pandemic.[26] To help leaders and managers prioritize self-care and create a caring culture, they can learn to nurture the dynamic of mindfulness, which plays another critical component of nurturing equanimity.

---

[23] Accenture. 2021. *The Future of Work: Productive Anywhere.* www.accenture .com/_acnmedia/PDF-155/Accenture-Future-Of-Work-Global-Report.pdf# zoom=40.

[24] Ibid.

[25] Ibid.

[26] A. Puravankara. October 10, 2021. "Why Companies Must Prioritize Wellness in the Workplace." www.weforum.org/agenda/2021/10/the-importance-of-worker-well-being-in-the-future-of-work/.

CHAPTER 6

Detailing the Two Paradigms of Mindfulness

While the first five chapters of this book examined the macro trends facing organizations in the post-COVID market, this chapter and the next four explain specific characteristics of a caring culture that nurtures equanimity. The first characteristic of a caring culture that nurtures equanimity is understanding the two paradigms of mindfulness. If the leadership team has supported the level of self-care required in a nurturing environment as discussed in the previous chapter, it can then help promote the cultivation of a healthy mind that involves mindfulness as explained from the east (the cessation of the fluctuations of the mind) and from the west (focus a calm concentration on the present moment). While there is much discussion of mindfulness in the business literature for managers and leaders today, the term is so often misunderstood, it requires its own chapter here. Once leaders and employees agree upon a shared definition of mindfulness, it can incorporate it throughout the organization as yet another way to nurture equanimity and build a caring culture. Another option available to leaders and managers focused on nurturing equanimity and creating a caring culture is to invite employees to practice both forms of mindfulness. In the post-COVID marketplace, whether an organization supports one definition or both, one thing is certain, those cultures looking to build a sustainable future will have mindfulness as an option to seriously consider as one element of an employee-focused work environment.

In an April 23, 2016 *The New York Times* editorial, Matthew E. May explained that there are two opposing approaches to mindfulness: Eastern (nonthinking) and Western (focused thinking).[1] Both approaches start

---

[1] M.E. May. April 23, 2016. "Achieving Mindfulness at Work, No Meditation Cushion Required," *The New York Times*. www.nytimes.com/2016/04/24/jobs/achieving-mindfulness-at-work-no-meditation-cushion-required.html.

with the individual, and since organizations are made up of any number of people, it is important to remember that, according to a new study published in 2022, the benefits of mindfulness do not end with the individual. According to Christopher S. Reina and other researchers, "The real payoffs emerge when an individual's mindfulness is translated into mindful interactions and relationships. Such interactions—infused with intentionality, compassion, and presence—can bring about more harmonious and healthy organizations."[2] Both May and Reina highlight the role mindfulness plays in helping people "actively think through problems in new ways to achieve innovative, elegant solutions."[3] The "mindful interactions and relationships" Reina mentioned are formed when one gains an understanding that a person's perspective is merely one among alternative views, and processing multiple perceptions requires one to embrace uncertainty. Mindfulness allows space for the acceptance of alternative views when discussing solutions to a business problem. This space then, when "infused with compassion," can help nurture equanimity and create a caring culture where employees foster a more harmonious and healthy relationship among themselves. The first approach to mindfulness that can help infuse one with intentionality, compassion, and presence is the Eastern view.

The Eastern view is more about quieting the mind and suspending thought and originates from the belief that "Yoga is the cessation of fluctuations of the mind," which is found in the second verse in *The Yoga Sutras of Patanjali*, an instructional text for classical yoga dating from somewhere between 5000 BC and 300 AD. *The Yoga Sutras of Patañjali* is a collection of 195 Sanskrit sutras (aphorisms) on the theory and practice of yoga. In Hinduism, sutras are a distinct type of literary composition, a compilation of short aphoristic statements; each one resembling a short rule or theorem distilled into few words around which teachings

---

[2] C.S. Reina, G.E. Kreiner, A. Rheinhardt, and C.A. Mihelcic. 2022. "Your Presence Is Requested: Mindfulness Infusion in Workplace Interactions and Relationships," *Organization Science*. https://doi:10.1287/orsc.2022.1596.

[3] M.E. May. April 23, 2016. "Achieving Mindfulness at Work, No Meditation Cushion Required," *The New York Times*. www.nytimes.com/2016/04/24/jobs/achieving-mindfulness-at-work-no-meditation-cushion-required.html.

of philosophy or other fields of knowledge can be woven. *The Yoga Sutras* was compiled in the early centuries CE by the sage Patanjali in India, who synthesized and organized knowledge about yoga from much older traditions. Patanjali, also known as Gonardiya or Gonikaputra, was a Hindu author, mystic, and philosopher. Scholars and researchers have confirmed very little of his identity as no one knows exactly when he lived. From an analysis of his works, however, it is estimated that it was between the 2nd and 4th centuries CE.[4]

How does one achieve *Yogash citta vrtti nirodha*, translated as *yoga is the cessation of the modifications, or fluctuations, of the mind?* To achieve this sutra or aphorism, one engages in the physical postures of a yoga practice. There are various forms of yoga to practice. Ashtanga, vinyasa, and yin are three of the most common. Each practice is made up of a series of physical postures or asanas—meaning seat in Sanskrit. Each practice, regardless of how demanding it is on one's physical structure, prepares an individual for the last pose. At the end of the physical practice, they should be able to quiet the mind and suspend thought with the goal to rest in a meditative state, also known as savasana, which is often the last pose. It is in that pose that one seeks to achieve the cessation of the fluctuations of the mind. Fluctuations of the mind includes all the thoughts, feelings, opinions, emotions, memories, misconceptions that barrage our existence on a seemingly endless cycle. Ceasing the fluctuations of the mind is extremely difficult work and often takes years of practice. The term "practice" is associated with yoga for this reason. One practices learning how to cease the fluctuations of the mind and does so throughout their life with the knowledge that it is a lifelong pursuit.

Closely associated with yoga and its pursuit of the cessation of the fluctuations of the mind are the eastern martial arts. Eastern martial arts tend to be closely associated with the spiritual traditions from which they originated. The practice of Japanese martial arts, such as archery, swordsmanship, and aikido, for example, share a deep connection with Zen Buddhist philosophy. The Zen concept of mushin ("no-mind-ness"), along with the nearly synonymous munen ("no-thought-ness"), is used by

---

[4] https://en.wikipedia.org/wiki/Yoga_Sutras_of_Patanjali.

instructors of these martial arts to emphasize the importance of removing mental interference during combat or competition. Sometimes translated as "unintentional," mushin refers to a state of consciousness that is free of intellectual deliberations or emotional disturbances of any kind. Another way of thinking about mushin is to consider a mind not fixed or occupied by thought or emotion and thus open to everything. It is translated by D.T. Suzuki as "being free from mind-attachment."[5] Throughout history, authors, philosophers, and scholars have written about the related impact of a no-mindedness state of existence. Eckhart Tolle and Alan Watts are two examples.

In his book *A New Earth: Awakening to Your Life's Purpose*, Eckhart Tolle explained how the phrase or mental state of "I don't know" is not confusion. The state of not knowing, according to Tolle should be reconsidered to "I don't know, but I should know" or "I don't know, but I need to know." This aspect of mindfulness can help you understand "When you fully accept that you don't know, you actually enter a state of peace and clarity that is closer to who you truly are than thought could ever be."[6] When you cease the fluctuations of the mind, you are able to nurture the self-care required to "fully accept that you don't know." In *The Wisdom of Insecurity*, Alan Watts echoed similar sentiment and described the acceptance of not knowing and its related insecurity as a characteristic of trying to be secure. For Watts "salvation and sanity consist in the most radical recognition that we have no way of saving ourselves. The principal thing is to understand that there is no safety or security." Thus, no-mindedness allows one the clarity of mind to fully accept there is no safety or security.

Becoming mindful within the paradigm of Eastern thought offers individuals a variety of approaches. Yoga, meditation, or a martial art can all help cease the fluctuations of the mind. Doing so takes years of practice and should be treated with the respect it deserves. Over time, one will be able to notice the mind at rest. This process of becoming mindful

---

[5] https://en.wikipedia.org/wiki/Mushin_(mental_state).

[6] E. Tolle. 2008. *A New Earth: Awakening to Your Life's Purpose*. www.amazon .com/New-Earth-Awakening-Purpose-Selection/dp/0452289963.

will allow one to have a greater sense of self-awareness. This increase in self-awareness will help one accept "there is no safety or security" (Watts) and "you do not know" (Tolle). In addition to the Eastern paradigm of mindfulness, leaders and managers of organizations looking to nurture equanimity and build a caring culture also have the Western view of mindfulness to consider. Such an approach involves "active thinking" compared to the "no-mindedness" of the Eastern paradigm. As Dr. Frank John Ninivaggi noted in an April 2018 *Psychology Today* article "Mindfulness in the West does not denote the traditional Eastern idea of emptying the mind wholly of all its objects or contents; instead, Western mindfulness aspires to a mind that can be alert and aware for significant times during the day."

Both views share the same goal: avoiding mindlessness. As May explained, "when we're mindless, the past is riding herd over the present. We get trapped in categories created in the past, stuck in rigid perspectives, oblivious to alternative views. This gives us the illusion of certainty." We convince ourselves that the present is something other than what it truly is. Other researchers would suggest mindfulness does even more. For example, Dr. Daniel J. Siegel echoes May's belief. Siegel, author of *Mindsight*, wrote "Research has proven that mindfulness training integrates the brain and strengthens the important executive functions that support emotional and social intelligence as well as academic success."

George Mumford, author of *The Mindful Athlete: Secrets to Pure Performance*, provides such an example and has been helping athletes understand how to stay in the moment. Mumford's backstory is quite interesting. He played basketball at the University of Massachusetts, but injuries forced Mumford out of the game he loved. The meds that relieved the pain of his injuries, however, numbed him to the emptiness he felt without the game and eventually led him to heroin. After years as a functioning addict, Mumford enrolled in Dr. Jon Kabat-Zinn's Mindfulness-Based Stress Reduction program and made meditation the center of his life. He kicked drugs, earned a master's degree in counseling psychology, and began teaching meditation to inmates and others. One example is the NBA team, the Golden State Warriors. The team is led by head coach Steve Kerr—who played for the Chicago Bulls during the

Michael Jordan era—and was taught meditation and how to refine the inner game by Mumford.

Under Kerr's leadership, the Golden State Warriors entered the most successful period in team history, reaching five consecutive NBA Finals and winning three championships in 2015, 2017, and 2018. The 2015–2016 Warriors won an unprecedented 73 games, breaking the record for the most wins in an NBA season, previously held by Kerr's 1995–1996 Chicago Bulls. Kerr explained how the four principles of competitiveness, joy, mindfulness, and compassion form the foundation of his coaching philosophy. In a professional sport where competition is ubiquitous and winning is judged on a daily basis, mindfulness plays a critical role in a culture where success is measured on both the player and team levels. According to Kerr, "If we can teach mindfulness, which is probably the biggest challenge of all in modern life, we can put all that together and teach our players perspective in how to perform under pressure."[7] Recognizing the need for self-care and its role in mindfulness, Kerr added: You have to nourish yourself. You have to fill up your own cup every single day to have the energy to lead others.[8]

With COVID, many organizations had no choice but to allow their employees to work from home since there was no going into the office. The emotional roller coaster COVID caused people tremendous stress, anxiety, and loneliness. Dr. Fortin of the Yale School of Medicine suggested one way to manage one's emotions is meditation. For those unsure of its practical application, Dr. Fortin recommended that people may find it easier to consider meditation as a gym for developing mindfulness. According to Dr. Fortin "In meditation, your only job is to follow your breath and notice what your mind is doing while that's happening. You'll then learn how to use the muscles you develop."[9] But mindfulness shouldn't be confused with other types of meditation such

---

[7] D. Sashin. May 13, 2021. "Warriors' Steve Kerr at Stanford Medicine Health Matters: Maintain Values in Times of Crisis," Stanford Medicine News Center. https://med.stanford.edu/news/all-news/2021/05/warriors-coach-steve-kerr-in-conversation-with-dean-lloyd-minor.html.

[8] Ibid.

[9] K. Katella. May 19, 2020. "Mindfulness: How It Can Help Amid the COVID-19 Pandemic." www.yalemedicine.org/news/mindfulness-covid.

as transcendental meditation (TM), a popular kind of meditation that involves using a mantra. Rajita Sinha, PhD, chief of psychology for the Department of Psychiatry and director of the Yale Stress Center noted a mindfulness practice does not necessarily involve meditation. "It is really about being in the moment, observing what's coming at you from the outside and what's coming up internally, taking it in and observing, and not reacting to it."[10]

After discussing which of the two forms of mindfulness the organization would like to nurture, leaders and managers then need to determine the best course of action required to implement such an important aspect of culture. Among the multitude of factors to consider are the length of the workday, work-from-home options, adequate break times, under-resourcing, off-hours e-mailing and correspondence, and micromanagement. If leaders and managers are serious about nurturing equanimity and creating a caring culture by offering mindfulness opportunities, the organization needs to offer adequate time for its employees to be mindful. Providing new and creative ways for organizations to support the physical, mental, and emotional well-being of their employees will continue to be a top priority for those leaders and managers interested in creating a caring culture.

Alexandra Croswell, assistant professor of psychiatry at the Weill Institute for Neurosciences at the University of California, San Francisco discussed the need for mindfulness to be a core skill for those leaders looking to nurture equanimity and build a caring culture. For Croswell, leadership should consider creating a culture that does not overwork their employees while implementing policies that support the physical and mental well-being of all employees. In a caring culture, then, there is little to no need for employees to use HR based tools, programs, or exercises to cope with work stress.[11] There is no need because the culture is such that employees find themselves in a caring environment and instead of trying to survive the organization, they are thriving in it.

---

[10] Ibid.

[11] M. Brammer. February 24, 2020. "Why Mindfulness Is Important to Organizational Culture," Dell. www.dell.com/no-no/perspectives/peace-keeping-why-mindfulness-is-the-future-of-successful-workplaces/.

In the post-COVID environment, organizations that seek a sustainable future will realize the observation of Reetika Gupta, deputy dean of Essec's APAC Business School, "acquiring talent is infinitely more expensive than retaining talent."[12] As organizations move forward in the post-COVID marketplace leaders will serve themselves and their employees well by leveraging equanimity and care to fundamentally change their culture for the better. Doing so will invite both forms of mindfulness and boost both employer morale and productivity. For example, employees who practice mindfulness are less bored at work and less likely to quit, according to a new study. Researchers including from the University of Exeter Business School found that in monotonous jobs, employees who are more "mindful" have greater job satisfaction, are less likely to quit, and think their job is less boring. However, mindfulness was found to boost the quality but not the quantity of work, in what the study described as a "double-edged sword" for task performance in monotonous jobs.[13]

Conclusion

A recent study in the *Journal of Occupational Health Psychology* revealed that people who practiced mindfulness during the workday showed reduced work–life conflict, increased job satisfaction, and an increased ability to focus their attention.[14] In a post-COVID world marked by continued fears of a global recession, inflation, and unstable political regimes, organizations would serve themselves well by creating a caring culture that helps employees reduce their stress through mindfulness.[15] To give

---

[12] "Being Kind Will Not Diminish Your Authority, Says Business School Leader." June 1, 2023. *CNBC*. www.cnbc.com/video/2023/06/02/being-kind-will-not-diminish-your-authority-says-business-school-leader.html.

[13] "Mindful Employees Find Their Jobs Less Boring and Are Less Likely to Quit." August 1, 2022. https://phys.org/news/2022-08-mindful-employees-jobs.html.

[14] J. Slutsky, B. Chin, J. Raye, and J.D. Creswell. 2019. "Mindfulness Training Improves Employee Well-Being: A Randomized Controlled Trial," *Journal of Occupational Health Psychology* 24, no. 1, pp. 139–149. https://doi.org/10.1037/ocp0000132.

[15] M. Brammer. February 24, 2020. "Why Mindfulness Is Important to Organizational Culture," Dell. www.dell.com/no-no/perspectives/peace-keeping-why-mindfulness-is-the-future-of-successful-workplaces/.

employees back time for mindfulness, or other activities, one such tactic some organizations are experimenting with is the four-day workweek. In the first large-scale assessment on the four-day workweek, none of the companies participating in the study plan on returning to a five-day week.[16] The survey tracked 33 businesses in the United States, Ireland, and Australia that cut an average of six hours from workers' schedules, with no change in pay, for 10 months and reported improvement in areas ranging from sales to productivity and well-being. Other findings from the study included:

- Workers on a four-day schedule were more inclined to work from the office than home.
- Employee absenteeism dropped from 0.6 days a month to 0.4, while resignations marginally dropped and new hires increased slightly.
- Companies rated the overall experience a 9 out of 10.[17]

As more organizations embrace the nurturing of equanimity through new initiatives like the four-day work week, a balanced remote work policy, and professional development opportunities, the more likely mindfulness as an aspect of culture finds its permanent place. This permanence, however, requires leaders and managers to engage in a consistent and positive approach to nurturing equanimity and creating a caring culture.

---

[16] C. Chapman. December 3, 2022. "Companies Embrace Shorter Workweek," LinkedIn News. www.linkedin.com/news/story/companies-embrace-shorter-workweek-5075129/.

[17] Ibid.

CHAPTER 7

Emphasizing Consistency and Positivity

Due to the dynamics associated with today's volatile, uncertain, complex, and ambiguous (VUCA) global marketplace, many organizations "were trying to reinvent their culture before the pandemic—partly to attract talent, but also, to drive innovation and future-proof the business."[1] Back in February 2020, Kevin Martin, chief research officer at the Institute for Corporate Productivity, observed the continuous disruption related to operating in a VUCA environment had become the new normal and called for organizations to evolve both their strategies and business models as well as their culture. As Paul McDonald noted in a *Forbes* article, the business, social, and cultural disruptions companies and their workers are experiencing now (post-COVID) are far more consequential than much of the digital or other types of change they previously confronted. Successful companies, McDonald argued, "understand that their organizational culture must continually evolve in response to change."[2] According to research findings published in the *2022 Organizational Culture Research Report* "65% of employees say their culture has changed in the past two years. While some organizations have successfully adapted to this new world of work, others have struggled to build, improve, and maintain company culture."[3]

Unfortunately, 23 percent of employees say their culture changed for the worse during the 2020–2022 period. While some organizations

---

[1] P. McDonald. June 25, 2020. "Why a Positive Company Culture Is Especially Critical Today," *Forbes*. www.forbes.com/sites/paulmcdonald/2020/06/25/why-a-positive-company-culture-is-especially-critical-today/?sh=a7273c52e5b8.

[2] Ibid.

[3] Quantum Workplace. n.d. *2022 Organizational Culture Research Report*. www.quantumworkplace.com/future-of-work/organizational-culture-research.

evolved and adapted after the onset of the pandemic, others fell far short in creating a caring culture. Inept, incompetent, or indifferent leaders and managers who were inconsistent or negative in their handling of one situation after another failed to adapt their culture and, as a result, placed their organization at a severe disadvantage. When a leader or manager is inconsistent or negative, it creates a culture of distrust, confusion, and disengagement. Employees need to know that their leadership can remain positive and consistently caring even during the most disruptive of market events. Research findings suggest 69 percent of organizations that adapted amid the pandemic say culture offers them a competitive advantage.[4] A consistent and positive evolution of culture that nurtures equanimity is paramount for those organizations looking to remain vital, vibrant, and relevant in today's hypercompetitive, ever-changing, and dynamic global marketplace.

Consistency is one of the strongest traits among the world's greatest leaders. Consistency, when coupled with positivity, provides the business, its employees, and stakeholders with a known quantity. And more than anything, people respect and admire consistent leaders. Additionally, according to Karolyn Hart, "The most loving thing a leader can do for their team is to be consistent."[5] Leaders and managers who have as one of their goals the evolution of organizational culture by nurturing equanimity often provide a high level of consistency since they realize it is unfair to the employees to keep them guessing.[6] A leader is someone who should be able to inspire confidence with everyone in the organization at all times, as opposed to someone who has momentary flashes of brilliance. When a leader is consistent, they are able to inspire trust, whereas a leader who is inconsistent can leave their charges reeling on a daily basis.[7] Gregory Roll of Touchpoint Associates emphasized the role of authenticity, consistency, and meaning when he said "People should

---

[4] Ibid.

[5] K. Hart. September 3, 2020. "The Most Loving Thing a Leader Can Do for Their Team Is to Be Consistent." www.inspirehub.com/blog/the-most-loving-thing-a-leader-can-do-for-their-team-is-to-be-consistent.

[6] Ibid.

[7] D. Chou. May 31, 2016. "Are You a Consistent Leader?" *CIO*. www.cio.com/article/238170/are-you-a-consistent-leader.html.

walk away from interactions with your business with a certain feeling. Focus on what you want and need that point of reference to be and how you can work to manage that outcome."[8]

Being consistent as a leader or manager comes down to self-awareness and a high level of comfort with one's humanity. Ultimately, being consistent depends upon the leader or manager being authentic as employees want to see the people they report to as one of them. As Steve Dion discussed, "Leaders who show their real and genuine selves to others at work build stronger bonds of trust." When applied in a consistent fashion over an extended period of time, this authentic leadership "provides the fuel to power their teams to tackle thorny issues with openness and transparency. Navigating times of change requires faith in others that are guiding them through unknown waters."[9] As Amy Cooper Hakim reminded leaders in a March 2023 *Forbes* article "leaders set the bar for the expected atmosphere and office climate at work. Remember that positivity breeds positivity."[10]

Matt Coleman concurred with Dion's observation about authentic leadership and the necessity of such an approach applied on a consistent basis when he wrote: "Great leaders I work with and have worked with have an ability to act, react, and make decisions in a consistent manner."[11] For Coleman, a leader inspires confidence and does so consistently. "When a leader is consistent, they are able to inspire trust, whereas a leader who is inconsistent can leave their team struggling on a daily basis."[12] As Scott

---

[8] "15 Simple Yet Effective Ways to Highlight Company Culture." December 12, 2022. Forbes Business Council. www.forbes.com/sites/forbesbusiness council/2022/12/12/15-simple-yet-effective-ways-to-highlight-company-culture/?sh=c2cfa835c6ae.

[9] S. Dion. February 11, 2022. "We Need Authentic Leadership More Than Ever in 2022," *Fast Company.* www.fastcompany.com/90717032/we-need-authentic-leadership-more-than-ever-in-2022.

[10] A.C. Hakim. March 21, 2023. "Are You a Positive Leader at Work?" *Psychology Today.* www.psychologytoday.com/us/blog/working-with-difficult-people/202303/are-you-a-positive-leader-at-work.

[11] M. Coleman. July 12, 2020. "The Importance of Constant Consistency as a Leader," LinkedIn. www.linkedin.com/pulse/importance-constant-consistency-leader-matt-coleman/.

[12] Ibid.

Kriz pointed out, "There is no one-size-fits-all leader, but a consistent leader is able to build a team that will stand behind that leader and fight for the company because they understand and respect their consistency."[13] In today's volatile, uncertain, complex, and ambiguous (VUCA) global marketplace, the dynamics of disruption to industries and organizations will continue to present the biggest challenges to sustainability and profitability. Therefore, those leaders who provide employees and stakeholders with a consistent leadership style do so with the intention of producing a certain level of comfort and certainty.[14]

Conversely, when a leader fails to act in a consistent manner, employees are left confused, uncertain, and ambiguous as to what to do. Such feelings distract an employee's time and attention and often have a negative impact on productivity. "If the leader were consistent, people would know how they are expected to proceed."[15] Consistency helps "team members know what they're walking into every single day rather than tiptoeing into the office, wondering if the boss is going to be in a happy-go-lucky mood or if they need to be bracing to survive an apocalypse. They can focus on their job."[16] In a post-COVID workd of constant change, having employees focus on their job is paramount to the future success of any organization. Consistency, when coupled with positivity, are two critical components for those leaders and managers looking to nurture equanimity and create a caring culture.

In her book *Practicing Positive Leadership*, Kim Cameron defines positive leadership as "the implementation of multiple positive practices that help individuals and organizations achieve their highest potential, flourish at work, experience elevating energy, and achieve levels of

---

[13] S. Kriz. July 31, 2016. "For Better or Worse: A Consistent Leadership Style Is Key to Success," *Fortune*. https://insiders.fortune.com/for-better-or-worse-a-consistent-leadership-style-is-key-to-success-25e71fcea78d.

[14] Ibid.

[15] M. Coleman. July 12, 2020. "The Importance of Constant Consistency as a Leader," LinkedIn. www.linkedin.com/pulse/importance-constant-consistency-leader-matt-coleman/.

[16] S. Kriz. July 31, 2016. "For Better or Worse: A Consistent Leadership Style Is Key to Success," *Fortune*. https://insiders.fortune.com/for-better-or-worse-a-consistent-leadership-style-is-key-to-success-25e71fcea78d.

effectiveness." Nurturing equanimity and creating a caring culture is certainly one positive practice available to managers and leaders. In a December 22, 2022 press release, MNP, one of Canada's leading professional services firms, identified the role of positivity as a character trait for leaders. To achieve any level of sustainability in the post-COVID marketplace, MNP explained that leaders need to build their team around a positive culture both unique and measurable. Such a culture helps to retain talent by making sure employees have a say in how work gets done. Creating a positive culture is "one of the best investments leaders can make in the organization's future prosperity."[17]

When managers and leaders engage in a consistent practice of positivity, the organizational culture is such that it encourages team members and employees to excel in the work. Positive leadership applied on a consistent basis nurtures equanimity, creates a caring culture, cultivates an empowering environment through communication, maintains a high level of accountability, and leverages emotional intelligence. Positive leadership sees the well-being of the individual human and the organization as prongs of the same fork. Therefore, creating positive work conditions for employees and building relationships through teamwork will help the whole company prosper.[18]

A consistent application of positive leadership is also an illustration of the organization's values. In times of crisis, this is particularly important. Karen B. Moore, Founder and CEO of Moore, a nationally ranked integrated communications and public affairs firm, discussed organizational values in a December 21, 2022 *Forbes* article. According to Moore, those organizations wishing to create a caring culture should work hard at becoming an environment "where employees trust you to both deliver difficult news and, in turn, receive it from them."[19] As Moore

---

[17] "Using Culture as a Tool to Build and Maintain a Strong Workforce." December 22, 2022. MNP. www.mnp.ca/en/insights/directory/using-culture-as-a-tool-to-build-and-maintain-a-strong-workforce.

[18] www.wrike.com/blog/understanding-4-ps-of-positive-leadership/#What-is-positive-leadership.

[19] K.B. Moore. December 21, 2022. "5 Rules to Succeed In Business," *Forbes*. www.forbes.com/sites/forbesagencycouncil/2022/12/21/5-rules-to-succeed-in-business/?sh=323680a6c6a1.

noted: "As a CEO, I would prefer to receive worrisome news early than let it fester and surprise me later. Demonstrate that when someone owns up to a difficult situation, you can start crafting a solution together."[20]

In a December 19, 2022 press release, PBS Academy's CEO Derrick Chang discussed the significance of having a positive culture when he said: "Culture is the air we breathe everyday—invisible, yet the very core of what is needed to function well."[21] By building a cultural foundation built on self-awareness, Chang stressed that a consistent and positive approach would create a caring culture "ensuring that staff wellness is well taken care of. It is important that we remain committed in supporting the well-being of our colleagues."[22] Chang highlighted two programs the PSB Academy implemented in 2022 to create a caring culture: a monthly inflationary assistance pay-out amounting to 4 percent of their gross monthly salary to assist them in coping with inflation and having off the last week in December. For Chang, giving employees that last week in December off "is a good way for them to pause, reflect and recharge."[23] In a December 27, 2022 *Psychology Today* article, Ronald E. Riggio discussed how strong and positive organizational cultures lead to growth and benefits for organizations.[24] According to Riggio, a consistent and positive leadership style can help organizations "weather the storm" during change or a period of disruption. Moreover, "research shows that companies focusing on a strong corporate culture see increased revenue, stock prices, net income, and job growth."[25]

Future evidence of the need for a consistent and positive workplace culture comes from analysis conducted by Sheila Callaham. According to her assessment, the most-read article on *Forbes* in 2022 was "Workplace

---

[20] Ibid.

[21] "Building a Culture Where People Matter—Here's How an Employer Supports Its Workforce Through Inflation." December 19, 2022, press release. www.yahoo.com/now/building-culture-where-people-matter-024900317.html.

[22] Ibid.

[23] Ibid.

[24] R.E. Riggio. December 27, 2022. "Company Culture: The Key to Fueling Leadership and Growth," *Psychology Today*. www.psychologytoday.com/us/blog/cutting-edge-leadership/202104/company-culture-the-key-to-fueling-leadership-and-growth.

[25] Ibid.

Culture: 5 Key Elements for A Positive Employee Environment." Callaham observed how the article resonated with readers because in the post-COVID environment, workplace culture is powerful and when crafted in a positive and caring manner, can be a significant factor in business success; and when done poorly, can create a dysfunctional environment that drains talent.[26] With culture impacting every employee, Callaham noted that leaders and managers need to recognize the significance of applying a consistent and optimistic perspective. Doing so can help recruit, engage, and retain employees.[27] The five key elements for a positive employee environment are belonging, contribution, flexibility, equity, and growth mindset. As Callahm concluded, "each of the five factors represents a strategic opportunity to better engage employees. Whether employers tackle just one or all five, employees are likely to respond favorably." [28] Further evidence of developing a positive organizational culture stems from research published January 2023 in the *Frontiers in Psychology* where researchers found that "To develop a positive organization, a leader needs to create positive assumptions among (and about) coworkers, positively impact the personal and professional development of employees, and balance positive formal and informal conditions at work."[29] The essential condition, or *sine qua non* as identified by the research team, is the "necessity of a positive leader to foster his/her personal development by exercising the virtues and developing practical wisdom."[30] When a leader demonstrates personal growth and development, "they provide followers with a vision of the final end towards the common good and achieves to set his/her organization on a pathway towards excellence."[31]

---

[26] S. Callaham. December 27, 2022. "Most Popular Articles Show Employers More Focused on Workplace Culture," *Forbes*. www.forbes.com/sites/sheilacallaham/2022/12/27/most-popular-articles-show-employers-more-focused-on-workplace-culture/?sh=7b5168185b42.

[27] Ibid.

[28] Ibid.

[29] D.M. Redin, M. Meyer, and A. Rego. January 4, 2023. "Positive Leadership Action Framework: Simply Doing Good and Doing Well," *Frontiers in Psychology*. www.ncbi.nlm.nih.gov/pmc/articles/PMC9848739/

[30] Ibid.

[31] Ibid.

Conclusion

In a December 18, 2022 *Forbes* article, Rhett Power noted the crucial role leaders play in creating organizational culture and wrote: "Leaders play a crucial role in defining and articulating the values, practices, and beliefs that will support the company cultures they aim to create. And leaders can fail at maintaining these cultures for various reasons."[32] Leadership styles grounded in narcissism, fear, insecurity, or cronyism are just a few of the common approaches leaders use and, as a result, fail at nurturing equanimity and creating a caring culture. Successful leaders, however, are self-aware and remain dedicated to nurturing equanimity for themselves as well as for those around them. They have the ability to acknowledge and embrace their individual approach, know what their weaknesses are, and hire complementary individuals who will compensate for those weaknesses. While this was true prior to the global pandemic, it is even more so today. Organizations that nurture equanimity and create a caring culture require a leadership and management team focused on providing a consistent and positive approach to the evolution of culture. For those organizations, however, that continue to lack a caring culture in 2023 and beyond, they risk, according to Richard Safeer in a December 9, 2022 article, "facing a full-blown human capital and workforce crisis. If companies and organizations want to be successful, which means having a viable and reliable workforce, the time to create a healthy and well workplace culture is now."[33]

In a February 17, 2023 *Forbes* article Justin Hale labeled the most important skill for leaders to have in the near future is to be "less strategy experts and more human experts." In the post-COVID workplace "leaders need to become experts in why people do what they do if they want to

---

[32] R. Power. December 18, 2022. "Here's How Leaders May Be Unknowingly Causing a Toxic Workplace," *Forbes*. www.forbes.com/sites/rhettpower/2022/12/18/heres-how-leaders-may-be-unknowingly-causing-a-toxic-workplace/?sh=65ed96212ca6.

[33] R. Safeer. December 9, 2022. "Employee Well-Being: Culture Is the Cure, Smart Brief." https://corp.smartbrief.com/original/2022/12/employee-well-being-culture-is-the-cure.

help their people act differently."[34] The pursuit of having employees act differently is a prerequisite in today's VUCA marketplace. The marketplace dynamics are changing and so should the organization, its culture, and people. A consistent and positive leader who understands human behavior can help change the behavior of employees, and as a result, drive outcomes in a positive manner. Leaders who are consistent and positive understand that if their influence is lagging, they should first look inward and not blame the employees. Doing so requires a strong sense of self-awareness among leaders. This ongoing pursuit for self-awareness and the corresponding need to evolve organizational culture will also require leaders and managers to maintain a growth mindset to continue to meet new challenges, disruptions, and issues related to today's VUCA environment. By prioritizing a growth mindset where the fundamental belief is hard work, persistence, and learning are what "produce results organizations can unlock the full potential of their workforce, creating a more diverse and adaptable team."[35] In addition to consistency and positivity, leaders who nurture equanimity and create a caring culture will also maintain and encourage a growth mindset.

[34] J. Hale. February 17, 2023. "The Most Important Leadership Skill for 2023," *Forbes*. www.forbes.com/sites/forbescoachescouncil/2023/02/17/the-most-important-leadership-skill-for-2023/?sh=61af685403f0.

[35] L. Freeman, Jr. April 17, 2023. "Developing a Growth Mindset Culture," *Forbes*. www.forbes.com/sites/forbesnonprofitcouncil/2023/04/17/developing-a-growth-mindset-culture/?sh=22de7e495822.

CHAPTER 8

Leveraging a Growth Mindset

In a December 30, 2022 article, Bobby Lewis emphasized the role organizational culture will play in 2023 and the immediate post-COVID future. According to Lewis, "organizational culture is a critical component of the workplace and nearly all the 3,000 full-time white-collar workers recently surveyed said company culture affects their decision to remain with their employer."[1] With the rise of remote work during COVID and then the subsequent escalation of hybrid work where employees only have to come into the office a few days each week or month post-COVID, Lewis noted, "it's even more imperative for employers to establish a comfortable and happy workplace environment."[2] As organizations of all sizes, industries, and locations continue to adapt to the post-COVID world in 2023 and find themselves navigating new employee situations such as hybrid work, consistent and positive leaders will need to rely on, develop, and enhance their growth mindset. With so many organizations leveraging some degree of a hybrid work model, leaders and managers will need to evolve as they learn how to deal with ambiguity. Of all the issues challenging organizations to remain vital, vibrant, and relevant, the continued and heightened sense of ambiguity is perhaps the biggest threat leaders and managers need to confront. To do so successfully, leaders and managers will need to leverage a growth mindset.[3]

---

[1] B. Lewis. December 30, 2022. "Refocus Company Culture," ATD. www.td.org/magazines/td-magazine/refocus-company-culture.

[2] Ibid.

[3] D. Morton. December 9, 2022. "Lessons Learned: Effective Leadership and Company Culture in a Hybrid Environment," *Forbes*. www.forbes.com/sites/forbestechcouncil/2022/12/09/lessons-learned-effective-leadership-and-company-culture-in-a-hybrid-environment/?sh=6b6855597d04.

As Derrick Morton noted in *Forbes*: "Ambiguity comes in many forms, from limited visibility into workloads to a lack of impromptu brainstorms and creative concepting. Leaders want to re-create the collaboration and camaraderie of the office while still encouraging the flexibility of remote work."[4] Recreating collaboration in a hybrid model, encouraging the flexibility of remote work, and creating a caring culture all require leaders and managers to challenge their own assumptions, think differently, and commit to lifelong learning.

Markus Edstrom, CEO, SFS Commercial Finance Americas, challenged his assumptions and upon reflection discussed how the COVID-19 pandemic crystallized what mattered most—the tremendous value of a positive company culture and the importance of our relationships with friends, family, and colleagues. Acknowledging how the pandemic induced virtual work taught him and his team the critical need for constant adaptability and digital tools, Edstrom now makes across Siemens, growth mindset a strategic priority across Siemens. By implementing the power of a growth mindset within Siemens he can further enrich its culture and allow the organization to create innovative and agile solutions to support customers. "A growth mindset will enable us to pinpoint clear objectives, develop a strategic plan to achieve these goals, and as I recently discussed with members of my team, will accelerate the digital transformation that we're working toward."[5] On the Siemens website is a list of the following six takeaways Edstrom had after reading Carol Dweck's *Mindset: The New Psychology of Success*:

- A growth mindset is about striving toward a higher purpose, with a mindset that change is constant.
- Growth-mindset leaders start with a belief in human potential and development-both their own and other people's.
- Growth-minded leaders offer an inclusive learning-filled, rollicking journey. "Becoming is better than being."

---

[4] Ibid.

[5] M. Edstrom. n.d. "The Influence of a Growth Mindset Post-Pandemic." https://new.siemens.com/global/en/products/financing/siemens-financial-insight-center/growth-mindset-post-pandemic.html.

- People with a growth mindset don't just seek challenge, they thrive on it.
- Use the approach, "this is hard, this is fun," when challenged with a task.[6]

In a December 8, 2022 article, Ralph Kilmann posed the question: "Why does one organization have a very adaptive culture while another has a culture that lives in the past? Is one a case of good fortune and the other a result of bad luck?"[7] Luck has little, if anything, to do with nurturing equanimity and creating a caring culture. Kilmann believed outdated cultures could be found anywhere leaders failed to manage culture explicitly in order to nurture it. Additionally, if an organization is growing in sales and size, it will be even more challenging to create and maintain a healthy company culture.[8] The operative phrase in his answer is "managed explicitly." Leaders and managers need to explicitly manage in such a way as to create a healthy workplace culture, and doing so starts with a growth mindset.

In a December 30, 2022 *Forbes* article, Cindy Jordan stressed the importance of a growth mindset. In her article "How CEOs Can Find The Right COO For Their Company," Jordan wrote: "A COO who is willing to learn, adapt and change to the needs of your business is critical. This flexibility gives you the ability to be nimble and react quickly to market changes." In today's post-COVID marketplace where disruption is common, Jordan observed how "the ability to maintain stability and consistency in your leadership team can be crucial to reaching the next level faster."[9] Moreover, leaders need to maintain a growth mindset as it will help them build what Deloitte labeled as "critical new

---

[6] Ibid.

[7] R. Kilmann. December 8, 2022. "Create and Maintain a Healthy Workplace Culture," *Mediate.* www.mediate.com/create-and-maintain-a-healthy-workplace-culture/.

[8] Ibid.

[9] C. Jordan. December 30, 2022. "How CEOs Can Find the Right COO for Their Company," *Forbes.* www.forbes.com/sites/forbesbusinesscouncil/2022/12/30/how-ceos-can-find-the-right-coo-for-their-company/?sh=555700456ad7.

competencies—leading through change, embracing ambiguity, and uncertainty."[10] Recognizing the need businesses have to hunt for increasingly agile skill sets to stay competitive, JD Dillon wrote, "leaders must find ways to provide flexible learning opportunities for a myriad of roles without substantial costs or administration so their organization can keep pace and demonstrate value."[11]

One illustration of a growth mindset comes from the words of Irish playwright George Bernard Shaw who wrote "People are always blaming their circumstances. I do not believe in circumstances. The people who get on in this world are those who get up and look for the circumstances they want, and if they cannot find them, make them." Those with a growth mindset understand they have the opportunity, at any moment, to change their circumstances by learning a new skill, improving their habits, or increasing their knowledge. In short, there is no limit to their growth. While Shaw has a point, it might be more exact to say that "the people who get on in this world" have a growth mindset. Individuals with a growth mindset are comfortable leaving their comfort zone since they understand doing so presents opportunities for development. Viewing obstacles as learning opportunities, cultivating your growth opportunities, and committing to lifelong learning are characteristics of a growth mindset.

In her 2006 publication *Mindset: The New Psychology of Success,* Carol Dweck concluded that people have either "fixed" or "growth" mindsets. In a 2016 *Harvard Business Review* article Dweck summarized the impact of organizational cultures that endorse, practice, and promote a growth mindset. For Dweck, individiuals who have a commitment to lifelong learning via a growth mindset do so through working hard, applying a high level of effort over an extended period of time, and receiving feedback from others willing to provide a critique of weaknesses and strengths. Her research discovered that growth mindset individuals tended to achieve more and out perform those with a more fixed mindset. Those with a fixed mindset believe their talents are innate gifts and therefore,

---

[10] 2019 Deloitte Global Human Capital Trends. n.d. "Leading the Social Enterprise: Reinvent With a Human Focus." www2.deloitte.com/content/dam/Deloitte/cz/Documents/human-capital/cz-hc-trends-reinvent-with-human-focus.pdf.

[11] J.D. Dillon. August 15, 2017. "In Real Life: Self-Directed Learning Can Only Work If…," *Learning Solutions.* https://tinyurl.com/yupf6ej5.

view self-improvement as a limited function of their natural abilities. To achieve any level of sustained growth in today's volatile, uncertain, complex, and ambiguous (VUCA) marketplace, cultures need to create a caring environment that allows individiuals to explore their growth mindset potential. When entire companies embrace a growth mindset, their employees report feeling far more empowered and committed; they also receive greater organizational support for collaboration and innovation. In contrast, people at primarily fixed-mindset companies report more cheating and deception among employees, presumably to gain an advantage in the talent race.[12]

For those leaders interested in nurturing equanimity and creating a caring culture, where growth mindsets are encouraged, the following exercise can help you determine your mindset. In each of the following 24 statements, select between two options, A or B, and then count how many of each you have.

A: I always want to look smart or talented.   B: I want to learn something new.

A: I never want to fail.   B: I am comfortable with failure.

A: I fear challenges.   B: I embrace challenges.

A: I give up easily.   B: I persist.

A: I blame others.   B: I take responsibility.

A: Giving up is the only option.   B: There must be another way,

A: It is good enough.   B: Is this really my best work?

A: This is too hard.   B: This may take some time and
effort.

A: I made a mistake.   B: Mistakes help me learn.

A: I just cannot do this.   B: I am going to train my brain.

A: I will never be that smart.   B: I will learn how to do this.

A: Plan A did not work.   B: There is always a Plan B or C.

If you selected B statements nine or more times, you have a growth mindset. If you answered B statements six to eight times, you have a mixed

---

[12] C. Dweck. January 13, 2016. "What Having a 'Growth Mindset' Actually Means," *Harvard Business Review*. https://hbr.org/2016/01/what-having-a-growth-mindset-actually-means.

mindset. If you selected B statements five or fewer times, you have a fixed mindset. Remember, one mindset is not better than another. Knowing your mindset will, however, help you increase your self-awareness as you continue to navigate the chaos and practice the art of living well. Dweck noted how difficult it can be for leaders to develop a growth mindset but observed "individuals and organizations can gain a lot by deepening their understanding of growth-mindset concepts and how to put them into practice. It gives them a richer sense of who they are, what they stand for, and how to move forward."[13] A recent case study of an organizational culture that failed to engage in a growth mindset comes from Southwest Airlines and the cancellation of thousands of flights during the December 2022 holiday season.

In a December 27, 2022 Facebook post titled "What happened to Southwest Airlines," veteran Southwest Airlines pilot of 35 years Larry Lonero wrote about the 2022 holiday disaster where thousands of Southwest flights were cancelled. His summary of his three-plus decades at Southwest is a case study on what happens when the organizational culture fails to develop a growth mindset. The culprit causing thousands of flights to be cancelled and, therefore, impacting holiday travel for tens of thousands of people was the antiquated computer system that handles scheduling for Southwest.

According to Lonero: "Unfortunately, the frontline employees have been watching this meltdown coming like a slow-motion train wreck for some time. And we've been begging our leadership to make much needed changes in order to avoid it."[14] Sadly, those changes were never made due to Southwest maintaining a culture generally resistant to change, ignoring frontline employees, and focusing on the rising stock price instead of necessary infrastructure upgrades. Noting the software's deterioration over years, Lonero said: "There was little investment in upgrading technology or the tools we needed to operate efficiently and consistently. As the frontline employees began to see the deterioration in our operation we began to warn our leadership."[15] But the leader-

---

[13] Ibid.

[14] www.facebook.com/photo/?fbid=623662526427797&set=a.296185345842185.

[15] Ibid.

ship failed to listen and, as a result, decades in the making, with one warning sign after another shot off like a flare gun lighting up the night sky, the Southwest system collapsed. Despite Lonero and his colleagues educating them (leadership), informing them, and making suggestions to them, the Southwest leadership and management teams ignored all pleas and dire warnings. Lonero ended his post with a reflection upon something the Southwest Airlines founder Herb Kelleher once noted and that is "'the biggest threat to Southwest Airlines will come from within. Not from other airlines.' What a visionary he was. I miss Herb now more than ever."[16]

Southwest, like any other organization that fails to implement a growth mindset culture, needs to understand that "in 2023, a cornerstone for all businesses should be building or maintaining a high-performance culture for substantial growth."[17] A high-performance culture needs to demonstrate to its people that it cares. Southwest Airlines failed to do that and ignored what frontline employees had been saying for decades. The end result was the opposite of a high-performance culture; it was a culture that crashed and now needs to find a way to rebuild itself while repairing its relationships with employees, customers, and partners. As Steve Arizpe wrote in a December 29, 2022 *Entrepreneur* article:

> A high-performance culture improves productivity, bringing higher profits and happier employees, improving talent retention, and continuing a growth cycle. A cornerstone of 2023 growth should be building or maintaining a high-performance culture for all businesses. Refraining or forgetting about culture in 2023 is a mistake, as it plays a critical role in company performance.[18]

---

[16] Ibid.
[17] S. Arizpe. December 29, 2022. "Why High-Performance Culture Is Critical to Business Success in 2023," *Entrepreneur*. www.entrepreneur.com/growing-a-business/why-high-performance-culture-is-critical-to-business/441040.
[18] Ibid.

Conclusion

To create a caring culture, it is imperative that leadership drive the change necessary for an organization to pursue a growth mindset. The leadership team "can incorporate a growth mindset into the organizational culture by promoting continual learning, accepting mistakes, and focusing on maximizing employees' potential."[19] As the dynamics of today's hyper-connected, ever-changing, and disruptive global marketplace continue to present new challenges to organizations across the globe, driving change through a growth mindset will become even more prominent. The increasing presence of Artificial Intelligence (AI) provides one example of many technological innovations forcing organizations to learn how to adapt in order to build a more sustainable future.

In a May 1, 2023 *Forbes* article examining the intersection of AI and a growth mindset, Michael Gale posits the question "where is the opportunity for individuals and organizations to make a difference with AI?" Recognizing that many people feel uncomfortable with AI, especially those who believe it will create a more dangerous future, Gale stressed that "AI is a growth mindset moment for every one of us. For those that design it and those that use and experience it."[20] Since AI will continue to add to the disruptive dynamics challenging the sustainability of organizations around the globe, it is imperative that leaders possess and promote a growth mindset among employees. With AI often described as an existential threat to humanity, a growth mindset is needed now more than ever for those organizations looking to remain vibrant, vital, and relevant in an ever-changing post-COVID global marketplace.[21] In order for organizations to achieve any level of a sustainable future in today's

---

[19] J. Johnson. March 22, 2023. "From the Classroom: A Strategy for Applying the Growth Mindset Concept to Your Business." www.business.com/articles/a-strategy-for-applying-the-growth-mindset-concept-to-your-business/.

[20] M. Gale. May 1, 2023. "Why Growth Mindset Is Needed With AI—10 Examples of Carol Dweck's Principles for an Existential Moment," *Forbes*. www.forbes.com/sites/michaelgale/2023/05/01/why-growth-mindset-is-needed-with-ai--10-examples-of-carol-dwecks-principles-for-an-existential-moment/?sh=4ea310d639c8.

[21] Ibid.

volatile, uncertain, complex, and ambiguous (VUCA) marketplace, leaders will need to shepherd breakthrough moments built on a growth mindset capable of driving chance. As Kent Ingle, president of Southeastern University noted "if you aren't willing to embrace change, you will reap the same results you always have. Learn to embrace a growth mindset by developing your leadership skills, seeking innovative solutions, and stepping out of your comfort zone."[22] One often overlooked aspect of a growth mindset is the acknowledgement of impermanence. Even a growth mindset understands humans have a finite amount of time alive. Leaders and managers who nurture equanimity to build a caring culture have the seldom discussed responsibility to help their employees understand the concept of impermanence.

---

[22] K. Ingle. April 21, 2023. "How a Growth Mindset Fuels Innovation," *Forbes*. www.forbes.com/sites/forbesbusinesscouncil/2023/04/21/how-a-growth-mindset-fuels-innovation/?sh=633436b22cc3.

CHAPTER 9

Acknowledging Impermanence

Building a caring culture requires everyone to acknowledge impermanence, as nothing is normal, static, or permanent. Work is fluid, job descriptions change, and even the mission of an organization is subject to alteration in today's dynamic, hypercompetitive, and ever-changing global marketplace. In today's volatile, uncertain, complex, and ambiguous (VUCA) global marketplace, leaders and managers need to understand themselves and help their employees realize what David Odell called "the impermanence of employment in today's connected, globalized world."[1] English writer William Somerset Maugham acknowledged impermanence when he wrote: "Nothing in the world is permanent, we are foolish when we ask anything to last, but surely we are more foolish not to take delight when it lasts."[2] In other words, stop thinking that life will get back to something called "normal" post-COVID, for normality has always been an illusion. The global marketplace in 2023 and beyond will never go back to "normal" because it was never that in the first place. Prior to COVID life was already disrupted by one VUCA dynamic after another. Author V.R. Ferose discussed impermanence in a *Forbes* article and referred to interviewing a job candidate who used the phrase "I am looking for a permanent position." Ferose astutely noted "The reality is, there is no such thing as a permanent position, there are only regular ones."[3]

---

[1] D. Odell. November 26, 2016. "The Impermanence of Employment," LinkedIn. www.linkedin.com/pulse/impermanence-employment-david-odell/?articleId=6208423855241908224.

[2] V.R. Ferose. March 20, 2020. "5 Ways to Design Our Lives for Impermanence," *Forbes*. www.forbes.com/sites/sap/2020/03/20/5-ways-to-design-our-lives-for-impermanence/?sh=3a679704b2ef.

[3] Ibid.

Leaders and managers who nurture equanimity and create a caring culture help their employees understand three tenets of impermanence: jobs, businesses, and products become extinct; massive layoffs happen far too often; and people frequently change jobs, industries, and even entire careers. Impermanence is found in everything from towns, schools, businesses, and jobs. Leaders and managers would serve themselves well by remembering that the management teams involved with now defunct businesses most likely believed their "normal" would exist forever and that people would rely on them their entire life. If the adage "what is past is prologue" is true, then as a leader or manager in today's post-COVID VUCA marketplace, help your employee acknowledge impermanence. Doing so might help the organization leverage its growth mindset and caring culture to remain vital, vibrant, and relevant. In no particular order, here are some extinct jobs, businesses, and products:

- *The milkman (job)*: Every morning in the 1950s, like clockwork, the milkman would deliver glass bottles and jugs filled to the brim with milk. In some cities and towns, the milkman also delivered other kitchen essentials like eggs and butter. With the advent and adoption of home refrigerators and freezers, the milkman became irrelevant.
- *The elevator operator (job)*: Originally, elevator operators were in charge of controlling everything from the doors and direction to the speed and capacity of the elevator car. In the 1950s, automatic elevators became more common, and individuals had to push their own button and, as a result, the elevator operator became extinct.
- *The bowling pin setter (job)*: In the early days of bowling alleys, the position of bowling pin setter went to someone who loved to be around games. The workers manually organized the pins for every game. This job became outdated once Gottfried Schmidt invented the mechanical pinsetter in 1936.
- *Blockbuster (store)*: Founded in 1985, Blockbuster was once the entertainment giant of the world, with more than 65 million registered customers and more than 9,000 stores in the United States alone. But the rise of streaming services,

digital content, and competition from other entertainment sources all had a negative impact on Blockbuster's profit margin. After 29 years in existence, Blockbuster filed for bankruptcy in 2014 with more than $900 million in debt.

- *Borders (store)*: Opened in 1978, the Borders bookstore became a staple for anyone looking to enjoy a shopping experience centered around reading. Sadly, the leadership and management at Borders failed to develop an online store and held on to too much stock in CDs and DVDs. After 33 years in existence, the last Borders bookstore closed its doors in 2011.

- *Circuit City (store)*: Opened in 1949, Circuit City grew into one of the top retail stores and helped pioneer the big-box concept of selling everything from televisions, computers, refrigerators, and so many other electronic products. In the 1990s, the leadership and management failed to maintain a caring culture and when coupled with the increased competition, the chain closed its last store after 60 years in 2009.

- *Typewriters (product)*: Even though it was around for centuries and used by people around the world, the typewriter has been relegated to a collectible item. As computers and printers were adopted around the world starting in the 1980s, the typewriter started to lose its relevance and, by the early 2000s, found itself collecting dust on a shelf, never to be used again.

- *Floppy disks (product)*: Once the only way to store data or install software, the floppy disk was introduced in the 1970s and grew in relevance over the next two decades. With the advent of memory sticks, downloading, and cloud storage, floppy disks eventually grew obsolete by the early 2000s.

- *Cassette tapes (product)*: From the 1960s to the 1980s, cassette tapes were an iconic image of storing, sharing, and recording music. When the Compact Disk (CD) was introduced in the 1980s, cassette tapes started to quickly lose their relevance. Of course, CDs would suffer the same fate as cassette tapes with the advent of digital music in the 2000s.

There are hundreds of other examples of positions, stores, and products once thought indispensable now obsolete. One common element uniting each of the positions, stores, and products in the aforementioned list is the advent of technology. As long as disruptive new technologies continue to be created and then adopted, impermanence will continue. No job, store, or product is safe from the rapid development of automation, artificial intelligence, or advanced technological innovations. Thus, a quick reflection upon the last century-plus of history and it becomes clear that rapid technological change and disruption have long been the rule, not the exception. Contrary to public belief, normal has never existed and it is doubted it will anytime soon. Categories of jobs once viewed as integral to Western economies have shrunk or essentially disappeared, only to be replaced by new ones. Such transformational dynamics, however, seldom stay within the United States or Western economics. Commenting on the constant rate of change and disruption in the workplace, Rhys Dubin stated that what happens the U.S. or West "seldom remains isolated for long and is often a harbinger for changes to come."[4] A glimpse into upcoming change comes from former Google CEO and executive chairman Eric Schmidt who commented in a May 2023 discussion on how a declining birth rate in the U.S. has all but guaranteed the continued rise to prominence of artificial intelligence in the workforce. "In aggregate, all the demographics say there's going to be a shortage of humans for jobs. Literally too many jobs and not enough people for at least the next 30 years."[5]

The obsession people have with permanent jobs is ill-conceived. Nothing is permanent. As Ferose observed, "nothing in the world is permanent? Not jobs, not relationships, not friendships, not our nationality, not our status, not life itself. We want things to stay exactly as they are. Because permanence feels like security."[6] In addition to

---

[4] R. Dubin. July 16, 2018. "There's No Such Ting as a Stable Career," *Foreign Policy*. https://foreignpolicy.com/2018/07/16/theres-no-such-thing-as-a-stable-career-jobs-employment-automation-economy/.

[5] "Life With AI." May 24, 2023. *Wall Street Journal*. www.wsj.com/video/events/life-with-ai/F13F8BDE-2AB5-4BA1-9191-997FC338C1AF.html.

[6] V.R. Ferose. March 20, 2020. "5 Ways to Design Our Lives for Impermanence," *Forbes*. www.forbes.com/sites/sap/2020/03/20/5-ways-to-design-our-lives-for-impermanence/?sh=3a679704b2ef.

the extinct jobs, stores, and products listed earlier, the second element demonstrating impermanence is the unfortunate realization that mass layoffs have always existed. Leaders and managers nurturing equanimity and creating a caring culture would serve their people well by helping them understand that unless their organization creates a sustainable business model and remains relevant, mass layoffs are always lurking around the corner as a last resort. A caring culture does not do this to scare its employees but instead to help them understand how organizations throughout history, that have failed to create a sustainable business model and remain relevant, found themselves facing extinction and with that, massive layoffs ensued.

This following list contains a brief compilation of the mass layoffs announced in 2023 alone. The people working in each organization, like employees everywhere, probably thought they would have their job for much longer. Their job was "normal" and the company needed them. They were hired, after all, in a "permanent" position. Remember, nothing is permanent and neither were any of the positions let go at the following companies:

- Rolls Royce mass layoffs: 6 percent of workforce laid off (May 2023)
- JPMorgan Chase mass layoffs: 500 workers of workforce laid off (May 2023)
- Paramount mass layoffs: 25 percent of workforce laid off (May 2023)
- Shopify mass layoffs: 20 percent of workforce laid off (May 2023)
- Morgan Stanley layoffs: 5 percent of workforce laid off (May 2023)
- David's Bridal layoffs: 83 percent of workforce laid off (April 2023)
- Roku layoffs: 6 percent of workforce laid off (March, 2023)
- Lucid Group layoffs: 18 percent of workforce laid off (March, 2023)
- Meta layoffs: 13 percent of workforce laid off (March, 2023)
- Twitter layoffs: 10 percent of workforce laid off (February, 2023)

- Twillo layoffs: 17 percent of workforce laid off (February, 2023)
- Roomba layoffs: 7 percent of workforce laid off (February, 2023)
- Disney layoffs: 3 percent of workforce laid off (February, 2023)
- Zoom layoffs: 15 percent of workforce laid off (February, 2023)
- Dell layoffs: 5 percent of workforce laid off (February, 2023)
- HubSpot layoffs: 7 percent of workforce laid off (February, 2023)
- PayPal layoffs: 7 percent of workforce laid off (February, 2023)[7]
- GrubHub layoffs: 15 percent of its corporate workforce laid off (June 2023)

The concerns for mass layoffs will continue into 2024 and the immediate post-COVID future. In a December 14, 2022 article, George Anders discussed the results of the latest LinkedIn Workforce Confidence survey and found that "31% of U.S. professionals are concerned their employers might be planning budget cuts and or layoffs."[8] To take matters into their own hands, millions of employees change their jobs, switch industries, or launch entirely new careers altogether each year. For those that change, there is nothing normal and they fully acknowledge the impermanence of life.

While the number of actual jobs people have throughout their lifetime fluctuates depending upon what generation is assessed, a 2019 survey by the Bureau of Labor Statistics (BLS) found that generally speaking, one person will hold about 12 different jobs throughout the course of their career. This number 12 is an average, however, and needs to be adjusted when examining different populations. For example, 40 percent

---

[7] "Mass Layoffs in 2022: What's Next for Employees," https://mondo.com/insights/mass-layoffs-in-2022-whats-next-for-employees/ and "Grubhub lays off 15 percent of its employees," https://www.engadget.com/grubhub-lays-off-15-percent-of-its-employees-190005627.html.

[8] G. Anders. December 14, 2022. "Breathing Easy: Worries About Layoffs Are Rarest for These 5 Types of Jobs," LinkedIn. www.linkedin.com/pulse/breathing-easy-worries-layoffs-rarest-5-types-jobs-george-anders/.

of Baby Boomers in the United States worked for the same employer for more than 20 years. Additionally, the BLS Employee Tenure Summary indicated that younger workers were more likely to switch jobs more often. Individuals aged 25 to 34 hold jobs for 2.8 years, those 35 to 44 for 4.9 years, 45 to 54 for 7.6 years, and 55 to 64 for 10.1 years. It does take a while for people under 30 to find a type of job, industry, or career path that may be of interest to them, so moving around is a natural explanation. Older workers may do so as a result of downsizing, layoffs, or simply wanting to do something different. Of course, there are many reasons why people leave one job for another.

According to one 2022 survey by FlexJobs, the number one reason people quit their job was a toxic company culture (62 percent). This was closely followed by low salary (59 percent), poor management (56 percent), and a lack of healthy work–life balance (49 percent).[9] Though a toxic culture is the biggest reason people leave their jobs, it's not the only reason people quit. These responses show that people want to work for companies with inclusive cultures no matter where they live or whether they work in-person, hybrid, or remote.[10] "Of the top seven factors people consider when deciding to quit a job, six of them revolve around the employee experience," Toni Frana, career services manager at FlexJobs said. "This speaks to how important it is to have a healthy company culture, with strong managers who really connect with and support employees."[11] Regardless of the reason, whether the individual is young and looking for a good career path, older and looking for something different, or simply fed up with incompetent leadership, one thing all workers who change jobs have in common is the fact that they are creating their own destiny.

The etymology of destiny is from the Old French meaning "to make firm or establish." What is it that you want to make firm or establish

[9] R. Pelto. March 2022. "Great Resignation: Survey Finds 1 in 3 Are Considering Quitting Their Jobs," *Flexjobs*. www.flexjobs.com/blog/post/survey-resignation-workers-considering-quitting-jobs/.
[10] Ibid.
[11] K. Dore. April 13, 2022. "Toxic Company Culture Is the No. 1 Reason Workers Are Quitting Jobs, Survey Finds," *CNBC*. www.cnbc.com/2022/04/13/toxic-company-culture-is-the-no-1-reason-workers-are-quitting-jobs.html.

with your life? Over the centuries, many authors have commented on man's search for destiny. Three recent authors are Herman Hesse, David B. Wolf, and John Kaag. German-born Swiss poet, novelist, and painter Herman Hesse explored an individual's search for authenticity, self-knowledge, and spirituality in his writings that included *Steppenwolf,* *Siddhartha,* and *The Glass Bead Game.* In 1946, Hesse received the Nobel Prize in Literature. On destiny Hesse wrote: "Each man had only one genuine vocation—to find the way to himself. His task was to discover his own destiny—not an arbitrary one—and to live it out wholly and resolutely within himself." A caring culture can help someone understand this. In 2008, David B. Wolf published *Relationships that Work: The Power of Conscious Living* and referred to a word closely related to destiny but one that has a richer history—dharma. According to Wolf: Dharma refers to "that which cannot be separated from a thing." He would go on to refer to fire as a way to envision dharma. "Fire, for example, can be used for different purposes, such as cooking. Cooking however is not the dharma of fire, because fire can exist without cooking. Heat is the dharma of fire. Heat is an intrinsic, inseparable quality of fire."

As philosopher John Kaag wrote in his 2018 book, *Hiking with Nietzsche: On Becoming Who You Are,* "The self does not lie passively in wait for us to discover it. Selfhood is made in the active, ongoing process, in the German verb, *werden,* 'to become.'" Hesse, Wolf, and Kaag each highlight the role of the individual in the development of one's destiny.

Conclusion

As Alyssa Satara wrote in an August 30, 2019 response to the question: "What are the lessons people most often learn too late in life?" She concluded that both the good and bad times are temporary. "We forget that it is about the journey not the destination. Everything is temporary, so make the most out of all of it." She reminds people to enjoy the good times and understand that the bad times are temporary when she wrote: "When you are up, enjoy it and be grateful for it. And when you are down, know you will get through it. Know that it is not the end, and that it is just a rough patch."[12] In a September 8, 2022 press release the consulting firm McKinsey provided evidence as to the impermanence surrounding workers and their jobs. According to McKinsey, many workers during COVID or immediately thereafter left entire industries. "Globally, only 35 percent of those who quit their jobs in the past two years remained in the same industry." Almost 50 percent moved to a new industry and under 20 percent choose not to return to work.[13] As the World Economic Forum reported in its 2023 Future of Jobs Report "in a survey spanning 44 countries, one in five employees reported they intend to switch employers in the coming year."[14] One critical take away this constant churn of workers demonstrated is the concept of unattachment. To nurture equanimity and create a caring culture, leaders have one other tool in their armamentarium and that is to encourage unattachment.

[12] A. Satara. August 30, 2019. "5 Lessons People Often Learn Too Late in Life," *Medium.* https://medium.com/the-ascent/5-lessons-people-often-learn-too-late-in-life-a69f27783864.

[13] McKinsey & Company. September 8, 2022. "Greener Pastures?" www.mckinsey.com/featured-insights/coronavirus-leading-through-the-crisis/charting-the-path-to-the-next-normal/greener-pastures.

[14] World Economic Forum. April 30, 2023. *The Future of Jobs Report 2023.* www.weforum.org/reports/the-future-of-jobs-report-2023/.

CHAPTER 10

Encouraging Unattachment

With the previous chapter outlining the many reasons why a leader or manager would acknowledge impermanence, this last topic marks the reasonable next step, and that is to encourage unattachment. A caring culture nurturing equanimity helps employees understand that while work is important, they should not be so attached to it that they lose their identity in their job title, function, or who they report to. Now this may seem contradictory since the entire concept of *Nurturing Equanimity: Building a Caring Culture* is centered around creating an environment conducive for people to both live and work, but the best leadership teams will develop their most talented individuals to develop their skills by encouraging them to move up in their own organization or, take on a new project, or if necessary, transition to a new position at another organization where they have a greater chance to flourish. This concept of being unattached relies upon a strong foundation from the previous step of impermanence. Organizations that desire to nurture equanimity and build a caring culture should help their employees understand that they should not get more attached to their work than their family or personal health. The research is overwhelmingly clear on this last aspect of a caring culture. Leaders should encourage unattachment so their employees can focus on what is truly important in their life and remind them it is not work. Failure to do so could cause significant harm to employees.

When the attachment between employee and employer becomes blurred and the individual fails to separate his identity from that of the organization, psychologists use the term "enmeshment." Enmeshment prevents the development of a stable, independent, sovereign sense of self. A caring culture that nurtures equanimity would surely have leaders and managers on the lookout for anyone of their employees suffering from enmeshment. In the post-COVID environment, leaders and managers demonstrating care toward their employees will need to encourage unattachment to prevent enmeshment, and in turn, doing so will help demonstration how the organization advocates for self-care. While enmeshment can happen at any level, it is often found in leaders and managers who encounter the confluence of high achievement, intense competitiveness, and a culture of overwork that catches many individuals in a perfect storm of career enmeshment and burnout. As psychologist Janna Koretz noted about enmeshment "these issues interact in such complex ways with people's identity, personality, and emotions that it often requires full-on psychological therapy to address them successfully."[1] There is a fine line to walk for those employees who intertwine their self-identify with their job. Doing so remains healthy if the individual remains unattached by actively engaging in a variety of interests outside of work. The danger lies in when the employee becomes so attached to their job that they lose interest in almost everything else in their life. When that happens, one is susceptible to an identity crisis if they burn out, get laid off, or even retire.

Koretz warned against the dangers of enmeshment and strongly urged individuals to add a dynamic other than work to their identity. With the closing of companies and collapse of entire industries embedded into the history of the global marketplace, an individual needs to understand how difficult it can be to find a job, especially for those in the mid to late stages of their career. "No matter how it happens, becoming disconnected from a career that forms the foundation of your identity can lead to bigger issues, such as depression, anxiety, substance use, and loneliness."[2] In her article "When You Lose Your Job—and It's Your Whole Identity," Rebecca Zucker echoed sentiment similar to Koretz when she wrote: "losing a job, regardless of an economic downturn or a restructuring—can seem catastrophic, causing an existential crisis."[3] In order to nurture equanimity

---

[1] J. Koretz. December 26, 2019. "What Happens When Your Career Becomes Your Whole Identify," *Harvard Business Review*. https://hbr.org/2019/12/what-happens-when-your-career-becomes-your-whole-identity.

[2] Ibid.

[3] R. Zucker. February 17, 2021. "When You Lose Your Job—and It's Your Whole Identity," *Harvard Business Review*. https://hbr.org/2021/02/when-you-lose-your-job-and-its-your-whole-identity.

and create a caring culture where employees are educated on the concept of unattachment to prevent employees from suffering from enmeshment or the "identity quake," leaders and managers have a valuable tool at their disposal through the research of Australian nurse Bronnie Ware.

Bronnie Ware is an Australian nurse who spent several years working in palliative care and caring for patients in the last 12 weeks of their lives. She recorded their dying epiphanies first in a blog that received a good deal of attention and then published her posts in a 2012 book called *The Top Five Regrets of the Dying*. Ware writes of the phenomenal clarity of vision that people gain at the end of their lives, and how we might learn from their wisdom. "When questioned about any regrets they had or anything they would do differently," she says, "common themes surfaced again and again." Here are the top five regrets of the dying, as witnessed by Ware:

- I wish I had the courage to live a life true to myself, not the life others expected of me.
- I wish I had not worked so hard.
- I wish I had the courage to express my feelings.
- I wish that I had let myself be happier.
- I wish I had stayed in touch with my friends.

The most common regret was "I wish I'd had the courage to live a life true to myself, not the life others expected of me." According to Ware, "this was the most common regret of all. When people realize that their life is almost over and look back clearly on it, it is easy to see how many dreams have gone unfulfilled." The second most common regret was "I wish I hadn't worked so hard." According to Ware, both male and female patients expressed this regret. "All of the men I nursed deeply regretted spending so much of their lives on the treadmill of a work existence." Academic research compliments Ware's findings from her experience. A Harvard study followed 268 undergraduates from the classes of 1938 to 1940 for 75 years, regularly collecting data on various aspects of their lives. The findings were reported in a 2012 book by Harvard psychiatrist George Vaillant titled *Triumphs of Experience: The Men of the*

Harvard Grant Study. According to the research, a happy and meaningful life consists of the following five elements:

- Loving relationships
- Money and power are small parts of a fulfilling life; they correlate poorly with happiness
- We can become happier in life as we proceed through it, despite how we started our lives
- Connection with others and work is essential for joy; and this seems to be increasingly true as one ages
- Coping well with challenges makes you happier

If an organization truly cares about its people and truly wants to nurture equanimity and create a caring culture, it will educate its employees about the research conclusions from Ware, Vaillant, and others. The evidence is overwhelmingly in favor of people who realize that work is but one component of a life well lived, and it should never come at the expense of one's personal health or family situation.

The concept of nonattachment dates to *The Yoga Sūtras* of Patañjali, a collection of 196 Sanskrit sutras (aphorisms) on the theory and practice of yoga. *The Yoga Sutras* were compiled prior to 400 CE by Patanjali in India, who synthesized and organized knowledge about yoga from much older traditions and introduced the concept of *Vairāgya* or nonattachment. Swami Niranjanananda Saraswati noted:

> The word "non-attachment" does not really exist in English, but it exists in Sanskrit in the form of *vairagya*, meaning to be free from attachment, without rejecting anything. It represents a state of mind that is continuously observing the nature of events and is unaffected. Non-attachment can easily be developed provided we can expand our awareness to see the reality behind things.

Vairāgya (वैराग्य) is a Sanskrit term used in Hindu that roughly translates as dispassion, detachment, or renunciation, in particular, renunciation from the pains and pleasures in the temporary material world. The Hindu philosophers who advocated *vairagya* told their followers that it is a means to achieve moksha (emancipation, enlightenment, liberation, and release). The word *vairagya* is composed of two words: *raga* meaning attraction and *vi* meaning not to be affected. *Vi* is a prefix which in combination with *raga* means "not being affected by attraction." "One interpretation of *vairagya* is that our consciousness is typically 'colored' by our attachments," wrote long-time yoga teacher Richard Rosen, "whether they are objects, other people, ideas, or other things." The attachments individuals have directly influence their sense of self and their relationships with others. Vairagya provides an individual with the opportunity to "bleach" or cleanse their consciousness of these attachments. This is not to say that people need to abandon possessions, friends, or beliefs. The practice of vairagya allows one to recognize the transitory nature of all of life and be ready to surrender any attachment at the appropriate time.

American actor Jon Hamm provides a modern-day example. Hamm was attached to his dream of acting and learned how to let it go. Both of Hamm's parents died before he was 21 years old. After graduating from the University of Missouri in 1993 with a Bachelor of Arts in English, Hamm returned to his high school to teach eighth grade acting. Attached to the desire to act for a living, Hamm moved out to Los Angeles with $150 in 1995. His older appearance made it difficult to find employment, and after three years, his agent dropped him. Still attached to his goal of acting, Hamm continued working as a waiter and set his 30th birthday as a deadline to succeed in Hollywood. His belief was that

> You either suck that up and find another agent, or you go home and say you gave it a shot, but that's the end of that. The last thing I wanted to be out here was one of those 45-year-old actors with a tenuous grasp of their own reality, and not really working much.

He gave himself permission to be nonattached to his dream and in doing so allowed things to happen. Soon thereafter, he landed the role of the advertising executive Don Draper in the AMC drama series *Mad Men*, which premiered in July 2007. The Draper role earned him a Golden Globe Award for Best Actor in a Drama Series in 2008. Reflecting back upon his experiences Hamm believes that "Losing both parents at a young age gave me a sense that you can't really control life—so you'd better live…all you can do is push in a direction and see what comes of it." American spiritual teacher Ram Dass wrote: "A feeling of aversion or attachment toward something is your clue that there's work to be done." Leaders and managers have a responsibility to their people to help them guard against the attachment between one's self-identity and work.

The evidence is overwhelmingly clear, leaders and managers have much room for improvement. For example, employee well-being and mental health take center stage amidst burnout and uncertainty, and businesses need to find ways to retain their employees and make them feel valued. According to a recent Gallup analysis, 52 percent of exiting employees say that their manager or organization could have done something to prevent them from leaving their job.[4] People leave jobs for all sorts of reasons, and it won't always be possible to keep every star employee. But with over half of the employees polled saying something could have been done to keep them, companies need to find ways to invest in their employees, from upskilling or tuition reimbursement to more creative and flexible compensation.[5] Nurturing equanimity and creating a caring culture should be priority number one for leaders and managers in the post-COVID environment. Doing so means changing the current culture.

Leaders and managers operating in the post-COVID environment of 2023 and the immediate future have to accept the frequency of organizational and cultural change. In today's VUCA marketplace, the management team of any organization looking to nurture equanimity and create a caring culture will make small adjustments along the way. A positive organizational culture helping employees understand the concept of nonattachment is a constant work in progress.[6] Although building a caring culture requires time and effort from managers,

[4] R. Frohwein. December 26, 2022. "The Future of Work: The 6 Biggest Workplace Trends in 2023 & Beyond," Benefits Pro. www.benefitspro.com/2022/12/26/the-future-of-work-the-6-biggest-workplace-trends-in-2023-beyond/?slreturn=20221127114010.

[5] Ibid.

[6] I. Shmidt. December 22, 2022. "How to Build a Strong Corporate Culture in Five Steps," Forbes. www.forbes.com/sites/forbesbusinesscouncil/2022/12/22/how-to-build-a-strong-corporate-culture-in-five-steps/?sh=230d10c15799.

HR staff, and all employees, the company could be rewarded with lower turnover rates, reduced retention costs, boosted productivity, and increased team morale. And now, as the pandemic has changed how teams work in so many ways, it's the perfect time for leaders to rethink how they run their organizations and start building truly amazing corporate cultures.[7]

In a December 15, 2022 *Forbes* article, Ali Davachi explained the significance of organizations to routinely "look within on a regular basis to determine whether their organizational culture is still effective or if they're drowning in dysfunction." It is nearly impossible for any organization 'drowning in dysfunction' to create a sustainable future. Davachi highlighted the challenges surrounding the results of any organizational self-assessment that identified change as an area of need. Implementing the required change to nurture equanimity and create a caring culture is never easy as "one study showed that only 18% of employees feel 'change agile.' Other research states that only 37% of change initiatives succeed."[8] Creating a caring culture is possible however if the leadership is willing to put in the required work. Kevin McGee, Anderson Valley Brewing Company, stated that one of the lessons he learned in 2022 was to embrace chaos, develop greater resilience, and learn how to become nimbler.[9]

Conclusion

In a January 1, 2023 *Wired* article, Kate Smale recognized the "cacophony of headwinds" facing organizations in the post-COVID market and noted the significance of culture in retaining talent. For Smale, organizations that create a caring culture focused on making their employees happy can

---

[7] Ibid.

[8] A. Davachi. December 15, 2022. "Transforming Company Culture: 4 Keys to Creating the Foundation for Change," *Forbes*. www.forbes.com/sites/forbes-booksauthors/2022/12/15/transforming-company-culture-4-keys-to-creating-the-foundation-for-change/?sh=56d0d7995fdb.

[9] "10 Business Leaders Share the Most Impactful Lessons They Learned in 2022." December 15, 2022. Rolling Stone. www.rollingstone.com/culture-council/panels/business-leaders-impactful-lessons-2022-1234644684/.

help the organization "move fast, create value, and maintain resilience."[10] To make employees happy, leaders and managers need to cultivate an intentional movement educating people on how to be good workers while maintaining an unattachment to the organization. Elliott Blodgett discussed the necessity of this intentional work in creating culture and wrote: "Culture will only grow if cultivated intentionally."[11] Blodgett recommended that leaders dedicate the required time and resources to achieve a culture built on authentic care. Leaders should "start small with team gatherings where the focus is on building relationships and trust. Throughout all of it, be open in your dialogue about the impact each of you has on your mission and values."[12]

Nurturing nonattachment is certainly one aspect of personal growth and professional development. While many organizations promise to develop their employees on some personal or professional level, Monique Valcour believes that such proclamations are "all too often that's just lip service. And it's up to managers to ensure their companies live up to the promises of professional development."[13] As Chief Marketing Officer of G2 Crowd, Ryan Bonnici makes sure his employees know he is serious about their personal growth and professional development. He even goes so far as to encourage them to secure a job elsewhere if they have learned everything they can at his organization. Bonnici embodies a leader who understands the significance of nurturing equanimity and creating a caring culture. Acknowledging the research finding that employees often quit not because of their company but because of their manager, Bonnici works hard at helping his employees achieve their personal and professional goals. As a result of such commitment, he noted: "I've had

[10] K. Smale. January 1, 2023. "Happiness Should Be the Most Important KPI for Tech Employers," *Wired*. www.wired.com/story/happiness-employment-labor-business/.

[11] "15 Effective Strategies for Maintaining Company Culture During Key Leadership Changes." December 26, 2022. *Forbes*. www.forbes.com/sites/forbescoach escouncil/2022/12/26/15-effective-strategies-for-maintaining-company-culture-during-key-leadership-changes/?sh=77564466354b.

[12] Ibid.

[13] R. Bonnici. September 11, 2018. "Why I Encourage My Best Employees to Consider Outside Job Offers," *Harvard Business Review*. https://hbr.org/2018/09/why-i-encourage-my-best-employees-to-consider-outside-job-offers.

employees tell me they chose to come work for me, and chose to stay, because of that commitment."[14]

In today's post-COVID global marketplace driven by volatile, uncertain, complex, and ambiguous (VUCA) dynamics where disruption is constant, leaders who seek to create a sustainable future for their organizations have the opportunity to nurture equanimity and build a caring culture. This publication provides a much-needed blueprint for caring leaders. By explaining the market realities (Chapter 1), articulating the strategic imperatives (Chapter 2), and linking personal and professional growth (Chapter 3), caring leaders form a strong foundation required of an organizational culture focused on equanimity and care. By defining equanimity (Chapter 4), prioritizing self-care (Chapter 5), and detailing the two paradigms of mindfulness (Chapter 6) thoughtful leaders highlight the dynamics of a caring culture. Finally, by emphasizing consistency and positivity (Chapter 7), leveraging a growth mindset (Chapter 8), acknowledging impermanence (Chapter 9), and encouraging unattachment (Chapter 10), responsible leaders exemplify the fundamental traits of an organizational culture that nurtures equanimity. These 10 steps are available to any leader who cares.

---

[14] Ibid.

Conclusion

In his April 2022 essay, "How to Stop Freaking Out," Arthur C. Brooks highlighted just how stressed and reactive Americans were as the country emerged from the pandemic. He provided the example of "air rage," where passengers become violent or unruly, that went from a typical 100 to 150 cases per year pre-COVID to more than 5,700 in 2021, most of which were mask related. Brooks then suggested "The problem is not limited to the skies. As my colleague Olga Khazan writes, 'disorderly, rude, and unhinged conduct seems to have caught on as much as bread baking and Bridgerton.'"[1] The level of stress continued throughout 2022 as Americans encountered inflation, politics, and global conflicts. As NPR noted in a December 22, 2022 press release, "Americans are understandably stressed and anxious about a range of things."[2] With this stress continuing for the foreseeable future into 2023 and beyond, it is no wonder that people have called for, in the words of Div Manickam, "Equanimity at work, life and everything in between."[3] Balance. People are seeking balance. In both their personal and professional lives people are seeking balance. With stress and anxiety continuing in the post-COVID environment, it will be up to leaders and managers to offer some relief at the workplace and to model the equanimity and care possible when humanity is prioritized in the organizational culture. Leaders need to care much more than they do today.

---

[1] A.C. Brooks. April 28, 2022. "How to Step Freaking Out," *The Atlantic.* www.theatlantic.com/family/archive/2022/04/how-to-manage-emotions-and-reactions/629692/?utm_source=pocket-newtab.

[2] R. Chatterjee. December 22, 2022. "Americans Are Under a Lot of Stress, But There Are Ways to Manage It," *NPR.* www.npr.org/2022/12/22/1145082601/americans-are-under-a-lot-of-stress-but-there-are-ways-to-manage-it.

[3] D. Manickam. April 25, 2021. "Equanimity at Work, Life and Everything in Between." https://divmanickam.medium.com/equanimity-at-work-life-and-everything-in-between-6ec1366c6c89.

In a December 18, 2022 article, Better Business Bureau CEO Steve J. Bernas commented on the role of culture and wrote: "a distinct company culture can help you develop a personality for your business that increases your authenticity among customers, which is an increasingly essential quality for reaching some key demographics."[4] Bernard Marr echoed a similar sentiment when he wrote in a blog post "in this era of declining trust, authenticity is a way for businesses and leaders to differentiate themselves. It's a way to build meaningful, lasting connections with audiences and employees alike."[5] This connection between authenticity and organizational culture should serve as a reminder to managers and leaders alike just how important nurturing equanimity is. Authenticity is difficult to create, maintain, and sustain in an environment that lacks equanimity. When organizations demonstrate a lack of care toward employees, clients, or other stakeholders, there is little chance of authenticity surviving. Employees at every level need to feel like they are being treated with humanity, compassion, and care. When employees get a sense that the organization is indeed concerned about their well-being, then authenticity can emerge as a component of the culture. This connection to authenticity through equanimity will continue to challenge managers and leaders in the post-COVID environment.

The ripple effects of COVID-19 on the global marketplace in general, and the workplace specifically, will continue as workers around the world continue to redefine their expectations of employers. In an October 20, 2022 *The New York Times* article, Emma Goldberg summarized why so many people were quitting and moving to another job when she wrote: "for many people, leverage meant the ability to create emotional distance from their employers, to draw stricter lines between who they are and what they do."[6] For those willing to make the leap, they created their own

---

[4] S. Bernas. December 18, 2022. "BBB Tips to Cultivate the Value of Company Culture," *Daily Herald*. www.dailyherald.com/business/20221218/bbb-tips-to-cultivate-the-value-of-company-culture.

[5] B. Marr. June 23, 2022. "Why Authenticity Matters and Every Organization and Business Leader Must Keep It Real."" https://bernardmarr.com/why-authenticity-matters-and-every-organization-and-business-leader-must-keep-it-real/.

[6] E. Goldberg. October 20, 2022. "Burned Out on Your Personal Brand," *The New York Times*. www.nytimes.com/2022/10/20/business/influencer-burn-out-jobs.html.

sense of equanimity and found an employer willing to respect such a need for balance. Fellow *The New York Times* writer Anna P. Kambhampaty told the story of several people and couples who quit their jobs during COVID. Researching into how they find their current life situation compared to their previous work experience, Kambhampaty found mixed results. For example, some people increased their salaries while others faced financial hurdles. "They've made it work by picking up part-time gigs on the side, giving up certain luxuries, or relocating to someplace less expensive. And despite the added stress, many feel that the decision was worth it."[7]

One person she interviewed was Ian Karle who quit a stressful job as a quality manager at a company in the oil and gas industry. Commenting on the impact quitting had on his quality of life, he told Kambhampaty: "You don't even know how much stress is on you until it's gone. It's ridiculous how much happier I am here than I used to be."[8] As more employees focus on their self-care, organizations that want to recruit, develop, and sustain human capital need to nurture equanimity and create a caring culture in 2023 and beyond.

In a December 29, 2021 *Forbes* article, Caroline Castrillon emphasized the year 2022 would be "the year of workplace culture." With an ever-increasing demand for recruiting, hiring, and retaining top talent, organizations dedicated to human capital emerged during the post-COVID environment with "a renewed focus on company culture."[9] With the pandemic's work-from-home mandate for many employees, individuals had to take on new roles, develop different skills, and learn to work differently. One benefit of this shift was that workers have started to emerge from the COVID isolation with a renewed emphasis on developing their skill sets. When an organization facilitates an employee's professional development, it "makes employees more valuable, it also gives companies a competitive edge. Another benefit is that workers who receive ongoing

---

[7] A.P. Kambhampaty. August 22, 2022. "How Quitting a Job Changed My Personal Finances," *The New York Times*. www.nytimes.com/2022/08/22/style/quitting-personal-finances.html.

[8] Ibid.

[9] C. Castrillon. December 29, 2021. "Why 2022 Is the Year of Workplace Culture," *Forbes*. www.forbes.com/sites/carolinecastrillon/2021/12/29/why-2022-is-the-year-of-workplace-culture/?sh=12cfbf3d1bbb.

training are more likely to stay with the company."[10] While competitive salaries, good benefits packages and flexibility are musts in the post-COVID competitive job market, leaders interesting in creating a caring culture should prioritize employee development as it "has some added advantages that truly make it a win-win proposition. From increased job satisfaction and loyalty to better retention rates—and ultimately better employees—continued learning benefits everyone involved."[11]

In other words, when an organization demonstrates that it cares about the people who work there, engagement and retention grow. Another way of considering this new trend is to rethink the oft-posed question: "Where do you want to work?" A better question to ask in 2023 by those leaders and managers nurturing equanimity and creating a caring culture is: "What unleashes a person's potential, enabling them to be healthy and productive, regardless of where they work?"[12] With more people entering the workforce post-COVID the question on what unleashes a person's potential will grow in significant. In its May 2023 jobs outlook report, the Bureau of Labor Statistics released its latest numbers and found "The share of people aged 25-54 in the workforce rose to 83.4% last month—the highest level since 2007."[13] In studying women in that same age range who are working or looking for work the BLS noted "the percentage rose to 77.6%, the highest level since the government started keeping records in 1948."[14] With more people entering the workforce, it behooves leaders to demonstrate care.

Building a healthy, effective, and cohesive culture, however, has become a lot more difficult in today's business environment. Due to the fragmentation, disruption, and dislocation of workers during the last few

---

[10] Ibid.

[11] J. Hall. February 26, 2023. "Why Businesses Should Invest in Employee Learning Opportunities," *Forbes*. www.forbes.com/sites/johnhall/2023/02/26/why-businesses-should-invest-in-employee-learning-opportunities/?sh=6842b9626154.

[12] Accenture. 2021. *The Future of Work: Productive Anywhere*. www.accenture.com/_acnmedia/PDF-155/Accenture-Future-Of-Work-Global-Report.pdf#zoom=40.

[13] Bureau of Labor Statistics. June 2, 2023. "The Employment situation—May 2023." www.bls.gov/news.release/pdf/empsit.pdf.

[14] Ibid.

years, organizations have struggled to maintain a cohesive culture across regions, business units, and work environments.[15] Employees in the post-COVID marketplace expect to have a greater say in the formation of the organizational culture. Leaders may indeed need to update their approach to creating culture and nurturing equanimity through care is an excellent start.[16] Back in 2016, and several years before the COVID's outbreak, Peter Vajda wrote the article "Why you need equanimity" where he recognized the need for equanimity in the modern VUCA world. Vajda understood the significance of equanimity as it "allows people to stand in the midst of conflict or crisis in a way where they are balanced, grounded and centered."[17] Vajda continued and noted how creating a sense of equanimity allowed individuals "to remain upright in the face of the strong winds of conflict and crisis, such as: blame, failure, pain, or disrepute—the winds that set us up for suffering when they begin to blow." In the post-COVID era, "the winds" of disruption will continue. Therefore, "equanimity protects us from being blown over and helps us stay on an even keel."[18] In a world of constant marketplace disruption, helping employees remain balanced is critical to a sustainable future.

Louis Camassa reminds leaders and managers of the obvious fact—every organization is made up of employees who are people first. People with feelings. People who would like to be treated with respect, kindness, and care. When those characteristics of a caring culture a missing, and leaders apply downward pressure to employees, for whatever reason, it creates an uncaring culture.[19] When employees know or feel that the management team bypassed them, belittled them, or pressured them into compliance, the culture takes an unprecedented downward spiral;

---

[15] D.L. Yohn. December 16, 2022. "Build a unified, Not a Uniform Company Culture," Smart Brief. https://corp.smartbrief.com/original/2022/12/build-a-unified-not-a-uniform-company-culture.

[16] Ibid.

[17] P. Vajda. March 4, 2016. "Why You Need Equanimity," *Management Issues*. www.management-issues.com/opinion/5992/why-you-need-equanimity/.

[18] Ibid.

[19] L. Camassa. December 13, 2022. "I Lacked This One Critical Skill That Nearly Cost Me My Career and My Life," *Entrepreneur*. www.entrepreneur.com/leadership/i-lacked-this-one-critical-skill-that-nearly-cost-me-my/435587.

nurturing equanimity is far from a possibility. An overwhelming amount of research suggests that empathy and personal interest increase employee loyalty and trust. In Harvard Business Review's Emotional Intelligence Series on Empathy, Emma Sappala writes how kindness and optimistic communications have more impact on performance than the number of zeros on an employee's paycheck. The author explains in another article that responding with anger or frustration erodes loyalty.[20]

In December 2022, Dale Carnegie and Associates released the results of a study conducted on organizational culture and concluded: "Leaders must consider workers' human needs right along with the needs of the organization. Flexibility and empathy will go a long way toward setting up employees—and the organizations for which they work—for meaningful long-term success."[21] Sadly, the abundance of workplace toxicity, the preponderance of incompetent leaders, and the overwhelming indifference by management have lowered the bar so much that the standard for 2023 and beyond is for organizations to remember to treat their employees as humans. Think about that for a moment. Although organizations have made great strides in one respect when it comes to culture, so much more needs to be done. One could argue that the COVID-19 global pandemic pressed the reset button, and many leaders have found themselves back at square one in figuring out how to manage people now that work has experienced a profound, and perhaps permanent, shift. In the post-COVID workplace, "if you want to attract and keep excellent employees, you must create and maintain a positive company culture."[22] My hope is that this book in some small way offers leaders and managers who care a blueprint on how to treat their employees as humans by nurturing equanimity and creating a caring culture.

---

[20] Ibid.

[21] B. Lewis. December 30, 2022. "Cultivate a Human-Centered Workplace," *ATD*. www.td.org/magazines/td-magazine/cultivate-a-human-centered-workplace.

[22] Bassam Kaado, "A Positive Company Culture Is A Top Priority for Job Seekers," *Business News Daily*, April 28, 2023. https://www.businessnewsdaily .com/15206-company-culture-matters-to-workers.html

Questions

The following list of 35 questions provides as a useful guide for those leaders who wish to engage in self-reflection on a few of the many topics raised in this publication. Nurturing equanimity and building a caring culture requires a leader to increase their self-awareness. Doing so can help them leverage their mind, body, and spirit as they work toward creating a sustainable future for their organization.

1. How often do you discuss the market realities with your entire team?
2. Who is responsible for providing updates on the market realities?
3. What discussions have you had lately about the changes in your marketplace?
4. What have you done lately to help employees understand the dynamics of today's volatile, uncertain, complex, and ambiguous (VUCA) marketplace?
5. What are your organization's strategic imperatives?
6. How often do you update the strategic imperatives?
7. Did your employees have any input into the strategic imperatives?
8. How often do you discuss the relationship between personal growth and professional development?
9. What have you done lately to grow as a person?
10. What have you done lately to enhance your professional skill set?
11. How often do you remind yourself if you want to grow as a professional you will need to grow as a person?
12. How often do you discuss the relevance of equanimity in your work place?
13. Does your organizational culture account for equanimity? If so, how?
14. When is the last time you emphasized equanimity to your employees?
15. What have you done lately to encourage self-care among your employees?
16. How often do you engage in self-care activities for yourself?
17. Has your self-care suffered lately? If so, why do you think that is?

18. How often do you allow your employees to engage in mindfulness?

19. What have you done lately to help foster mindfulness among your employees?

20. How often do you engage in mindfulness exercises?

21. How do you know if you are consistent in your management approach?

22. Do you consider yourself a positive leader? If so, how would you know?

23. What have you done lately to demonstrate your commitment to a consistent positive management approach?

24. What is the last new idea you considered or learned?

25. How committed are you to a growth mindset?

26. How often do you encourage your employees to have a growth mindset?

27. How often do you acknowledge impermanence?

28. Do you remind your employees that there is no such thing as a permanent position, product, or industry?

29. What have you done lately to help your employees prepare for change since nothing is permanent?

30. How often do you help employees recognize the need for them to be unattached?

31. How often are you balanced, grounded, and centered?

32. If you are not balanced, grounded, or centered, why do you think that is?

33. How often are you upright in the face of strong winds today?

34. How do you deal with conflict and crisis?

35. As a leader or manager, what have you done lately to create a caring culture where employees feel they work in an organization that will "stay on an even keel" during times of crisis?

About the Author

Michael Edmondson, PhD, is the author of seven Business Expert Press books. He has taught at a number of institutions of higher education including Rider and Drexel Universities and has served as a dean and campus director at New Jersey City University. He holds a PhD from Temple University and is the recipient of many awards and honors, including a Distinguished Leadership Award from the Monmouth, New Jersey, Regional Chamber of Commerce and an Entrepreneurial Inspiration Award by the Philadelphia Empowerment Group for his work with minority entrepreneurs in that city. Dr. Edmondson also sits on the board of the National Association of Continuing Higher Education and has completed the program at the AGB Institute for Leadership and Governance in Higher Education.

Index

OTHER TITLES IN THE HUMAN RESOURCE MANAGEMENT AND ORGANIZATIONAL BEHAVIOR COLLECTION

Michael J. Provitera, Barry University, Editor

- *11 Secrets of Nonprofit Excellence* by Kathleen Stauffer
- *The Nonprofit Imagineers* by Ben Vorspan
- *At Home With Work* by Nyla Naseer
- *Improv to Improve Your Leadership Team* by Candy Campbell
- *Leadership In Disruptive Times* by Sattar Bawany
- *The Intrapreneurship Formula* by Sandra Lam
- *Navigating Conflict* by Lynne Curry
- *Innovation Soup* by Sanjay Puligadda and Don Waisanen
- *The Aperture for Modern CEOs* by Sylvana Storey
- *The Future of Human Resources* by Tim Baker
- *Change Fatigue Revisited* by Richard Dool and Tahsin I. Alam
- *Championing the Cause of Leadership* by Ted Meyer
- *Embracing Ambiguity* by Michael Edmondson
- *Breaking the Proactive Paradox* by Tim Baker
- *The Modern Trusted Advisor* by Nancy MacKay and Alan Weiss

Concise and Applied Business Books

The Collection listed above is one of 30 business subject collections that Business Expert Press has grown to make BEP a premiere publisher of print and digital books. Our concise and applied books are for...

- Professionals and Practitioners
- Faculty who adopt our books for courses
- Librarians who know that BEP's Digital Libraries are a unique way to offer students ebooks to download, not restricted with any digital rights management
- Executive Training Course Leaders
- Business Seminar Organizers

Business Expert Press books are for anyone who needs to dig deeper on business ideas, goals, and solutions to everyday problems. Whether one print book, one ebook, or buying a digital library of 110 ebooks, we remain the affordable and smart way to be business smart. For more information, please visit www.businessexpertpress.com, or contact sales@businessexpertpress.com.

www.ingramcontent.com/pod-product-compliance
Lightning Source LLC
Chambersburg PA
CBHW061326220326
41599CB00026B/5056